FRESH
AIR

ALSO BY PETER DOWNIE

Healers at Work

Peter Downie

FRESH AIR

The Private Thoughts
of a Public Broadcaster

Northstone

Editor: Michael Schwartzentruber
Cover and interior design: Margaret Kyle
Cover photo: Tim McKenna
Consulting art director: Robert MacDonald

Permission:
"He's Only A Cat," from *Everything Arrives at the Light*, by Lorna Crozier,
used by permission of McClelland & Stewart, the Canadian Publishers.

Northstone Publishing Inc.
is an employee-owned company, committed to caring for
the environment and all creation. Northstone recycles, reuses and composts, and
encourages readers to do the same. Resources are printed on recycled paper and more environ-
mentally friendly groundwood papers (newsprint), whenever possible.
The trees used are replaced through donations to the Scoutrees For Canada Program.
Ten percent of all profit is donated to charitable organizations.

Canadian Cataloguing in Publication Data
Downie, Peter.
Fresh air
ISBN 1-896836-08-9
1. Downie, Peter. 2. Canadian Broadcasting Corporation –
Biography. 3. Broadcasters – Canada – Biography. 4. Broadcast
journalism – Canada. I. Title.
HE 8689.9.C3D68 1997 384.54'092 C97-910442-4

Published by
Northstone Publishing Inc, Kelowna, British Columbia

Printing
9 8 7 6 5 4 3 2 1

Printed in Canada by
Transcontinental Printing Inc, Peterborough, Ontario

A Dedication

This is for my dear father Tom and mother Doreen.
Both knew too little happiness in life and left
before I could understand.
It is also dedicated to Barb, Gord, and Bruce,
whom I love more than they know.
They have given me much happiness and now, at last,
they may have an easier time figuring out
what their brother's been up to for the last 25 years.

CONTENTS

PREFACE

You may have already heard, but just in case you haven't – the reports of my death as a public broadcaster are, unfortunately, not exaggerated. In my new "civilian" status, I can now discuss the state of affairs – mostly sorry – at the CBC with a freedom I haven't felt in over 25 years. But I confess I take no joy and only small comfort from this liberation. Although I no longer "live" there, it will always feel like home and I care for it dearly.

A man who taught me a great deal and was instrumental in my early career was Peter Gzowski, who, as I write these words, has just stepped down from hosting *Morningside*. Peter didn't become who he was, nor the program what it was, because of some panel or even a particular story.

Peter became an institution and an important symbol in this country because he communicated with each of us and he did it in a way which was easy and inviting. Producers and armchair theorists can and do go on endlessly about *this* aspect or *that* approach. Like the unique Barbara Frum on the television side, Peter *spoke* to us. End of analysis.

And that's all *I* ever wanted to do. There are times I can't quite believe that I've spent more than half my life trying to do just that at the CBC. To watch as it is systematically dismantled from the inside and from the outside by myopic bureaucrats and politicians has been a wrenching experience.

I have vanished into the Quebec countryside and have watched this spring as the farmer who owns the land this house sits on works it from sunrise to sunset. The transition involved in leaving the CBC and building a life outside of it has me feeling a bit like the freshly planted field behind the house – on some days full of potential while on others run over by a tractor.

If it is true that neutral people are the devil's allies, then what follows is, without question, the Lord's work. I believe too much in the ideals of public broadcasting to sit in silence and watch them frittered away.

So first, I simply add my voice to the chorus calling for the CBC – mostly television – to return to its roots, to rediscover the "public" part of its mandate, and to be true to all of us who want something *different* on the radio dial or television channel.

I don't know that there's much hope left for *public* television in Canada. By that I mean television which is driven by content and a dedication to fundamental non-commercial and alternative principles. If we ever get such a service in Canada, I'll be at the front of the line of supporters, shouting my encouragement, cheering it on. But that day is a long, long way off and I doubt whether there is the will or, more tragically, the management ability to rescue CBC television.

It has become an Edsel stuck in the passing lane on the Autobahn.

As with all large corporations in trouble, the people paying the price for the budget cuts and, at times, breathtakingly incompetent management aren't the managers. It's the poor sods who actually make the programs who pay by either losing their jobs or being told they now have to do five of them because their co-workers have been let go.

I would love to revisit television on occasion, but I know that it's not a place where I am ever going to feel at home. Like Calgary. I think television is more powerful and far reaching than we even know, and largely misused. When I became the host of the long-running and respected program *Man Alive*, I distinctly remember feeling that if I had to work in television, this would be the best it would get.

Perhaps that made the revelation of how *Man Alive* and the medium itself really worked that much more jarring. The truth is, by the time I left my last job in television, I had lost much of my faith in it – and in the CBC, which was, to me, far more troubling and disappointing.

I have found, especially since leaving, fewer and fewer people who watch CBC television. The current crop of American wannabe's running the network has committed the unpardonable sin of making the service largely irrelevant. Hardly anyone, except those who get a pay cheque from it, really cares anymore whether CBC television survives. And that's a shame.

But it has dug its own grave by presenting endless hours of prime time programming dedicated to juvenile comics, flash-in-the-pan sensationalism on once proud current affairs programs, stupid American situation comedies, and on and on.

A publicly funded network which airs *The Fresh Prince of Bel Air* and at the same time cancels performers like Tommy

Hunter and Rita MacNeil is so profoundly out of touch with the audience one is left to wonder who it's trying to impress.

CBC television has sold out and if it can't or won't become a *public* and *Canadian* service, it deserves to be shut down. Period.

And while CBC radio is, at the very least, a Canadian service, it seems to me that it has less and less justification for its smugness. I concede, with great reluctance, that the apparent emphasis on the part of the radio network to attract a younger audience is understandable and perhaps is even seen as a demographic necessity.

My experience was that public broadcasting is an *acquired* taste and so I'm worried more about what's lost through the current philosophy than what might be gained. *Definitely Not the Opera* is a cute name for a radio program, but I find the flippant attitude behind such a title insulting to all those who value the Metropolitan Opera broadcasts.

This is not snooty. I never listen to the opera on CBC radio Saturday afternoons, but I take comfort as a public broadcaster in knowing it is there. The whole purpose of public broadcasting, for me, is to stand apart from the rest of the dial by offering a unique product.

As well done as *Definitely Not the Opera* may be, in most parts of the country it is no longer unique on the radio dial. And I don't mean to single it out. It just feels to me like we – oops, *they* – have managed to alienate long-time CBC listeners for a quick hit with a younger audience which might very well soon find more of what they want somewhere else.

I have lived most of my life outside the major cities of this country and so I know only too well that CBC radio in "the regions" remains a life-line. That's precisely why I find it heartbreaking to watch it slowly and inevitably lose out to the central control of Toronto. There are times when Toronto gets so carried away with presenting a kind of theoretical content, I want to remind it that the "B" stands for broadcasting.

Radio is about communication, which leads to a shared experience. There's nothing magical about it. It is one person talking with and to another in a manner which is listenable. I don't turn the radio on to hear some-*thing*, I turn it on to listen to some-*one*.

I'm not sure how we've reached this point, just that we are there. Writer Robert Fulford once said a few years ago that he had plenty of friends who could recite the Broadcast Act back to front but didn't have a clue about what was actually on television the night before.

The CBC is top-heavy with people who can talk about what it is doing. I'm afraid that the skills of the people who can sit down and *do* it are not the ones much valued any longer. But this is not a phenomenon exclusive to the CBC, or even the media in general.

I asked my doctor recently how he was doing. For the next 15 minutes he never mentioned medicine, just the endless bureaucratic snafus and headaches involved in practicing these days.

I've just spent weeks trying to trade in my truck for a smaller car. It's astonishing to me that what the car dealers now spend all their time and energy selling is the financing. Almost no one has mentioned anything about the blessed automobile.

Applying for a mortgage today, as you probably know, has nothing to do with community and family and personal character. If the numbers which enter the computer are agreeable, you get the mortgage. If not, you're out of luck, although you might be a perfectly worthwhile risk.

The truth is, that attitude from banks and car dealers doesn't hurt them, but if you're in the business of relationship and community and trust, it can't get *you* very far.

When we raise this kind of technical information and ideas over practical *know-how* and *experience*, we're losing something very important – the passion, emotion and feeling which make us human. I think the absence of those things is acutely obvious in a medium like radio, when all you have is based precisely on them.

One of the signs of trouble which flows from this absence of real communication, and one which I have fun listening for, is when an announcer on the radio sitting in the studio by himself will say something like, "And we'll ask our listeners what they think...." Well, who in the world do they think they're saying that to? Knowing how to turn the microphone on is no guarantee you're speaking to anyone.

The CBC is in more serious trouble right now than it's ever been and, for the first time in 25 years, I fear for its future. I've said it before and will repeat that I think the choices being made now by the network are wrong.

If you cut off the regional strength and presence of the corporation across this country, the centre will soon wither and die. Disinterest is lethal. And I wish my old friends and colleagues, struggling through this seemingly endless crisis, nothing but the best.

My own "job" started over 25 years ago in a classroom in Fredericton, New Brunswick, when I encountered a man caught up in the noise of a war from the other side of the world.

In some respects, my "work" in life has begun largely because of a nun whose wisdom comes also from the other side of the world. But unlike the war we too often manufacture in life, hers is a peaceful wisdom which rests and breathes in silence.

Albert Schweitzer was asked once why he would want to give up his comfortable life in Europe to work with the sick people of Africa. He's quoted as answering that he wanted his life to be his argument.

I have spent a good and rewarding chunk of my life meeting people who are making "strong arguments" with their lives. Part of me now wants to try making one of my own. I'm still sifting through and setting aside the pieces I want to use in building *my* argument, but I've noticed how one element appears again and again in the stories of the men and women who have taught me in some way over the years.

I realize that while they all share an honesty, some have arrived at different truths. As a result, they have taught me something valuable about complexity and tolerance and of the priceless quality of simply deciding to take that first step on what must be a singular journey. You now hold the result of my first step in your hands.

The idea for this book came from a conversation with David Cleary and I thank him for giving *it* shape and *me* confidence. His enthusiasm is contagious. My longtime friend Gary Katz took some late night, early morning, mid-afternoon, weekday, and weekend anxious phone calls to help me sift through memory to find what really matters.

I especially owe my thanks to editor Mike Schwartzentruber, whose belief that this was a worthwhile effort is matched only by the care he took and the skill he gave to make it so.

ONE

"WELL,
IF I CAN'T PAINT ..."

At the height of the Vietnam war, when you'd have expected him to have other things on his mind, United States Army Chief of Staff General William Westmoreland took time out to convince me to become a journalist. Well, not intentionally, but the flash of anger and contempt that swept across his face and the narrowing of his glare as he lined me up in his sights started me thinking that asking questions and poking the powerful might just be an interesting way to make a living. And so it was for the next 25 years of my life.

I came to learn that asking a question can sometimes feel like pulling the pin on a hand grenade. Appropriately enough, I pulled the pin on my first ever little "hand grenade" during a question and answer session of a military history course at the University of New Brunswick. The '70s had just begun, the Vietnam war wouldn't end, and here was General Westmoreland standing amidst the stately elms and the lovely serenity of the U.N.B. campus.

Fredericton is one of my favorite places in the world, but it's not exactly a mecca for newsmakers. And so I'm still not sure if the appearance of this imposing figure said more about his personal war weariness back on the home front or about the connections of our professor. Whatever the reason, I was eager to ask Westmoreland about an interview I'd read with an American soldier who had called him "the biggest bastard ever to set foot in Vietnam." An opinion I shared, of course, without any serious knowledge or even thought.

Given the times, who could have possibly doubted that America was in fact the true Evil Empire? Armed with considerably more hair than awareness, we despised everything American, except necessities like Boone's Farm Apple Wine.

I'll take refuge now behind the idea that being young allows one to be right for the wrong reasons. As we've since learned, it's just possible that "bastard" is one of the kinder and gentler terms that could be used to describe General Westmoreland as Commander of American forces in Vietnam between 1964 and 1968.

Had I only politely asked for a comment, my life might have been completely different. I would quite probably be farming somewhere on the eastern end of P.E.I., writing about raising sheep and endangered species of farm animals, contemplating the beauty of Cape Breton rising on the horizon across the misty gulf. But nooooooo. With only the arrogance of youth rising on the limited horizon of a student, I asked him how it felt to actually *be* "the biggest bastard ever to set foot in Vietnam." As much as I now know that listening is *the* big secret of successful broadcasting, I can't remember what Westmoreland replied. Back then, it didn't matter.

What *did* matter was that for a fraction of a second, I caught his attention. True, I was the proverbial mosquito swatted aside indifferently by the giant elephant, but by God, I left that classroom a new and energized mosquito, suddenly and unexpectedly addicted to the sweet blood drawn by a well-timed, pesky question.

But it didn't take long to understand that if I tossed a question like a hand grenade at someone experienced in this kind of warfare, I had to be prepared to duck or fight the subsequent "incoming." That meant, I would learn, that a completely different agenda was suddenly in play – one that had far more to do with egos than it did with substance.

Long after I had left that classroom and joined the ranks of the media, one of the decisive moments I remember most clearly regarding ego and the tossing of verbal grenades happened during a television interview in a Toronto hotel room with U.S. presidential candidate Gary Hart. You need to remember that we had all just seen the endearing vacation photograph of Senator Hart with Donna Rice bobbing along in the big, blue sea near the Bahamas.

Hart and I had been having what I thought was a pretty good conversation. I'm a political junkie and I think he appreciated that. While it wasn't likely we'd be shipmates any time soon, the comfort level between us made me brave enough to switch gears. The question went something like this: "Considering all your experience with the media and presidential politics, and as a reflective, smart guy who knows the ambition and singlemindedness necessary for a run at the White House, why in the world would you ever even get *on* a boat called *Monkey Business*?"

It's not easy to find the words to describe what happened next, but let me say that part of the life which flashed before my eyes was the memory of playing hockey on the streets of Montreal, when a frozen tennis ball would hit in the wrong place, when all you could do was drop to the ground in a fetal position, gasp for air that tasted like road salt, and madly pray that death in the form of a truck would come quickly.

The black-hole-like suction needed to empty that hotel room of its oxygen propelled Mr. Hart forward and, as he leaned in, I shuddered from the sudden Arctic cold front whistling through my soul. In my mind's eye, the front axle of that merciful truck was almost over me. My knees knocked, my heart pounded and the chiseled features of Hart's face suddenly became liquid, as if Salvador Dali had gone berserk, transforming the famous face before my eyes like a wax figure caught in a fire.

In the next split second, Hart's body language became aggressive and my first thought was, "Oh my God, he's actually going to hit me." My second thought was, "Well, at least *Midday* will get a little attention," and my final thought was, "I wish Valerie had done this interview."

Hart's blue eyes froze and through his now impossibly tightened jaw, he almost whispered, "*That* I will not answer."

"It's time to get up off the road and go back home," is what I thought. It was a valuable lesson which led to the fairly obvious conclusion that I was just not very good at or comfortable with going for the sound bite or the jugular – a legitimate style of interviewing, but certainly not mine.

It seems to me that to put someone in front of a microphone and ask for the viewer's or listener's valuable time and attention, and to then fight like schoolyard kids is a waste of everybody's time and energy. It becomes a kind of theatrical cock fight.

Don't misunderstand – I had (the past tense here is more hope than fact) a large enough ego to want to be the centre of attention for so many years and to be the filter through which the day's news would pass. It's going to take even longer for me to lose such a silly motivation and to understand how that paradox is at the heart of my ambiguity toward today's media, or more accurately, ME-dia.

You need what could charitably be called a "healthy" ego to think that anyone would actually want to listen to or watch what you have to say in the first place, but, as in other areas of life, ego blocks meaningful relationship and communication. I love ideas and the word artistry of spirited conversation, but to turn a radio microphone or television camera into ego extensions and instruments of intimidation in "battle" just bores me silly.

This "gotcha" approach to journalism may regrettably be necessary for the newscast every night, but I just don't have it in me to spend time aiming at the next target that pops up in the shooting gallery that is the daily news. This, of course, has been dressed up in the elaborate costumes and the fancy language of million dollar anchors, but let's be straight about this – television news today, actually most of television, is about ratings and delivering an audience to advertisers. It is about nothing else.

You know, it's not that long ago that it *was* different. There was a time when journalists *didn't* fancy themselves stars, and television wasn't the great polluter. I've always believed that journalism, on its good days, is about searching for truth and about holding those in authority responsible for their actions.

When practiced with care and skill, journalism can still be an honorable and noble calling, but there seems so little honor and nobility left in the wake of television's almost complete cultural dominance. One of the more graphic descriptions of this came from a prominent Pulitzer prize-winning American author and teacher who chooses his words very carefully. He offered to me, in a whisper, that the equally prominent American news anchor who had visited his home the day before was nothing but a "high-class whore." He said this to me as we were on camera, but without audio. When the *Man Alive* episode went to air, I wondered what the viewers at home would think if they only knew what raised my eyebrows as he and I walked across his front lawn!

The result of all this is that I'm increasingly uncomfortable, embarrassed and honestly just bored watching those of us in the media become so self-important, practically prancing and preening across the world stage as if the television camera gives us a divine right to intrude, invade and insult everyone's privacy. I remember being "caught" twice, stopped in my tracks.

Once, I was sitting with a man whose wife and child had been killed in the aftermath of a bungled aircraft hijacking, when authorities stormed the plane on the ground and, in a horrible firestorm, killed some innocent passengers. This fellow, as I recall, was on his way to Ottawa to lobby for some future measure to deal with this kind of tragic situation.

In the "set-up" piece before our interview, as he and I sat inches from the monitor, we showed footage of the plane on the ground as it and his wife and child were consumed by this fiery explosion. I understand how and why this dramatic, compelling footage got there, but as the eyes of this proud, strong man welled with tears, I was ashamed by what we had done.

I was equally angry with myself after sitting down with the Soviet dissident Natan Sharansky, soon after his famous walk to freedom across the Glienicke Bridge to West Berlin in 1986.

You may remember that his wife, Avital, had campaigned around the world with a fierce devotion for his release.

Now he was a free man sitting across from me and I asked if he ever, in the morning over coffee and the newspaper, looked at her and wondered to himself if or how he was ever going to be able to adequately repay her. He answered quickly: "Some things should remain private." And I knew he was right.

James Carville, the eccentric and brilliant strategist behind Bill Clinton, usually hurls words around with the force of a tornado, but not when it comes to television. He simply calls it "the Monster," which must be cared for and fed day in and day out. That's true even when the White House *isn't* up for grabs.

But I'm missing whatever genetic make-up it takes to be part of that food chain. I'm unable to stick a camera or microphone in someone's face and virtually demand an answer. And I understand how, when faced with the "Monster's" insatiable and indiscriminate appetite, people and places and things become essentially the same and nothing more than food.

Most of the people I met in television are smart. They're not inherently cynical or unfeeling. But the easiest thing to sacrifice, while juggling all the demands of the medium, is perspective. A few years ago, a friend in Montreal began working as a television reporter and I watched the newscast one night as a story was presented about how the police had discovered and finally hauled a body out of the St. Lawrence River.

When the camera showed this plastic wrapped, lifeless lump being dragged up the bank of the river to land, there was one person caught virtually running out of the shot. It was my inexperienced friend, mistakenly reacting like a normal human being. Her days as a reporter were numbered.

Our "times" speed past us now in an almost unrecognizable blur. Murder trials appear on the entertainment channel and images of starving children are followed by pictures of people stampeding each other to buy "Tickle Me Elmo"® dolls at K-Mart. Most television has the intensity of a greeting card, and more and more I think Oscar Wilde was right when he said that instead of monopolizing the seat of judgment, journalism should be apologizing in the dock.

As proof of my single-minded devotion to the media for the past quarter century, I've actually been surprised to discover that huge chunks of important life go on without a camera or microphone anywhere in sight. That's only a slight exaggeration and a clear indication of just how narrow my vision had become.

It was not until I stepped away, particularly from television, that I found a new life, feeling a powerful and growing discomfort with the media's taste for black and white simplicities.

As Voltaire wrote in 1770, "While doubt is never a pleasant condition, certainty is absurd." Let me tell you this: "Francois-Marie Arouet Voltaire Live" ain't likely to get the go-ahead on *Newsworld*. And so, in the end, I think I just grew weary of a job which fed my ego and starved my self-respect.

Of course, I didn't have a clue about any of this in 1968 when I arrived at the University of New Brunswick with the intention of studying Political Science. My media awareness up to that point consisted of having watched way too much *Bonanza*, *Ed Sullivan*, *Dick Van Dyke* and *Lucille Ball* – okay, and sometimes *Queen for a Day*. As I think of that time now, television seemed just so ... well, innocent.

The year was 1968. What a time to begin a media career: Dr. Martin Luther King Jr., Bobby Kennedy, and Soviet tanks thundering into Czechoslovakia. The coverage of those events seems in retrospect to have been so restrained, almost limited, by today's standards. Think of actually having to *wait* for the latest news.

Today, CNN's cameras would have alerted the brave souls of Prague to the imminent change in "seasons," just as they signaled the moves of the Chinese government to the youngsters of Tiananmen Square. Who knows what impact that might have had on the course of history, and who that kind of power is attracting now to the business?

When John Kennedy was gunned down in Dallas in 1963 the only video of the event was taken by amateur eyewitness Abe Zapruder who only intended, of course, to record a home movie of the young president, not a piece of history. Today, we would surely have a Zapruder-like record of 1968's assassinations available around the world on the Internet and on CD-Roms, likely before the blood could be washed from that kitchen in Los Angeles or from the floor of that balcony in Memphis.

At the same time this medium is becoming so dominant in our lives, we surely become more aware, as we grow older, that meaning in life comes at least as much from context as it does from our individual decisions and actions.

Amnestic television endangers that awareness with its constant onslaught of images, blurring together to deliver a kind of instant history where nothing but the present matters. Like a fish flapping in the bottom of a boat, we're left in this new media world, gasping for the contextual air that sustains and informs our lives. With television as big "Daddy," kids kill other kids for running shoes and life becomes what happens between commercials.

But, as I said, in 1968 when I walked into CHSR (College Hill Student Radio) at the University of New Brunswick, this was unimaginable. In fact, I recently found an old flyer, which we must have handed out on the campus, with the headline "WE'VE GOT IT ALL TOGETHER ..." On the inside, we went on to boast of our "Tri-campus sound of service, serving 3000 students in all U.N.B. residences, St. Thomas University, N.B. Residence Co-op, Teacher's College and the Student Union Building."

In truth, I spent most of my time at the station and not in the classroom, and my claim to fame from this period came about when the director of the radio station and I decided to raise funds for some charity by capitalizing on this predisposition. Over the period of a few days, I became the "Shaggy Dog." The deal was that I was supposed to stay on the air, without sleep, for a given period. If I didn't make it, I promised to cut off all my hair.

I don't remember how long I lasted, but I know I didn't get a haircut. And that friend and radio director, Bill Akerley, went on to great success, not to mention his own sleepless nights, as executive assistant to the president of the CBC.

The only thing I ever wanted to be when I was growing up was an artist and despite the nagging problem that I can't paint, the constancy of this dream has always been strangely comforting to me.

One of my earliest and fondest childhood memories is of a time when my father took me to the home of one of his favorite seascape artists, a man named Joseph Arentz, in Kennebunk, Maine. I must have been about eight at the time and was just astonished when Mr. Arentz showed me this vivid scene he had painted, covering an entire wall of his dining room. Bless my late father for not discouraging me when I announced on the way home that I was going to be a painter.

My concern with finding what to do for a living at such a tender age illustrates well, if not prophetically, the story of a radio executive who spoke to a bunch of youngsters. When one of the children announced that he wanted to work in radio when he grew up, the executive replied, "Just remember, you can't do both."

Oddly enough, when I was 31, in the last conversation I had with my father before his sudden death in 1982, I was as excited as that eight-year-old kid to tell him that I had signed up for a two-week art lesson in Kennebunkport that summer.

My father loved art, maybe because he saw beauty as the exception in life. I think he would stumble upon it, almost with surprise, and hope that those glimpses might be like bread crumbs on a trail he could follow back to his heart.

As I get older and further along the road of my own journey, I am reminded that I am indeed my father's son and that those rare moments when it seems possible to make sense of life have become my "bread crumbs."

Unintentionally, my interest and role in the media has declined in direct proportion to the importance of the discovery of those crumbs, but I haven't forgotten the inspiring promise of community and worthiness that radio offered in the beginning, along the gentle shores of the Saint John River.

TWO

THE POWER OF COMMUNITY

My first paying job in radio was with CJCJ, the proud home of "Frisky Fiddlehead," in Woodstock, New Brunswick, about an hour's drive west of Fredericton along the Saint John River valley. While its shores are gentle, the river sometimes isn't. During its more rebellious moments, I learned how radio could literally be the heartbeat of the community, pumping out critical, even life-saving information to those in distress.

If the flooding was bad enough in and around Woodstock, electric power could be lost, the bridges washed out, and the highways closed. Farmers faced the very real danger of their cattle being left stranded on higher ground.

Also, there was – and still may be – a more urban danger faced in Fredericton. For 11 months and two weeks of the year, the beautiful Beaverbrook Art Gallery enjoys its spectacular location, nestled serenely beside the river. But the spring "break-up" could also describe the nervous condition of the staff of the gallery, which stores two-thirds of its collection in the basement. I don't know if they've yet found a way to avoid the problem of flooding, but when I was around there was always dramatic springtime scrambling.

Even a painfully green rookie like me could figure out in a minute that this was not radio as background or simple companionship. The service we provided took on an urgency and a meaningfulness, if I can put it that way, that wasn't often repeated during the rest of the year.

Often, we'd stay on the air around the clock during this unfortunate spring ritual, relaying information to the victims and the threatened among our neighbors. In philosophical and practical ways, it shaped my outlook as a young, developing journalist.

I recognized, early on, that while the flooding conditions made our job more important, they also made *us* feel more important, a human factor you should never underestimate when assessing the news. In the absence of natural or manmade calamities, the media kicks into a self-preservation mode and must, by itself, elevate a story to importance.

A large part of every ordinary media day, led by television, is about reassuring, feeding and stroking the "Monster's" ego. Once it decides on "The Big Story," it has the means of making it *seem* like "The Big Story," and in the subsequent self-congratulatory process, descends upon it like sharks after blood in the water. Except sharks can't simply create at will their next victim and keep it bleeding. This is television's specialty. Ask Richard Jewell, falsely accused of planting a bomb during the Olympic Games in Atlanta, about swirling sharks.

The media, constantly starved for something dramatic and ever fearful of an ordinary day, can ruin the life of someone caught in its web without missing a beat. I recall watching Richard Jewell attempt to leave his apartment one day and make his way through the pack of media which had gathered by his door like hyenas around a fresh carcass in the Kalahari desert. Some dope screamed, "Why aren't you answering our questions?" I had my fingers crossed that Jewell would turn and politely respond, "Why are you *asking* them?"

There is a shameful zeal, bordering on the obscene, in the media's excitement over misfortune. It has nothing to do with gathering the news, as the tiresome refrain goes, and everything to do with an arrogance that tramples everyone and everything in its self-important path.

One of the tragedies of television's dominance in our society is that it has become the major way through which we validate our experience. When Marc Lepine's madness sent him on his insane crusade and he killed 14 women at the Ecole Polytechnique in Montreal, I remember the comment of one woman who appeared on *Man Alive*. She said that she didn't truly understand what she had just been through until she got to a friend's place and saw it on TV.

She wasn't talking about the details or the magnitude of the attack, which understandably she wouldn't have known. She meant the experience wasn't real until she saw it on TV. The tragedy is in the fact that this validation only flows one way and television will spit you out the second it can move on. It's constantly and methodically pulling the rug out from beneath us.

I think I was never comfortable with television work because I caught the bug about community involvement and media responsibility from those early experiences in New Brunswick. As far back as I can remember, I was inoculated with the idea that radio could play a substantial role by reflecting a neighborhood to itself and by assisting dialogue between the parts of a community.

It's a shame today that the idea of a radio station actually having a local presence and a responsibility to the community in which it operates is vanishing across the country. Relatively cheap syndicated programs from the United States increasingly fill the airwaves of Canada's private broadcasters.

A local station can now be run from the hard drive of a computer stored in a room no bigger than a closet, miles and miles from the community the station pretends to serve. And precisely when CBC radio is needed as never before, it abandons its role across the country. But I digress.

While these changes affect many communities across the land, they also have implications for aspiring broadcasters. When I began my career in radio, it was, well, *possible* to begin a career in radio. Going to a small town radio station as a rookie broadcaster and learning everything about the business by actually doing it was like starting out in the minors as a young hockey player, fueled by the dream of playing in the NHL. With hockey expansion, opportunities have grown for aspiring players. In radio, opportunities have shrunk.

A private radio station manager bragged to me recently about how a six hour announcer's shift could now be finished in about 20 minutes. Technology allows the announcer to come in, record the sterile links between music and commercials and go home; the computer programs the shift. The promise of a smaller payroll and, theoretically, fewer *human* mistakes has turned local radio into road kill on the technological/information highway.

Yet those inevitable human mistakes have made for some of the best moments of my career, or at least the most memorable. And I think they were tolerated by a very patient audience that was used to the parade of characters preparing for greater challenges, coming and going on their radio dials.

In my day, the challenge was getting to a centre like Halifax or Montreal, and it was reasonably assured that those stations would eventually need new blood from the "minor leagues."

But now a young broadcaster, say, in Sydney, Nova Scotia, has to compete against some cheap, whizbang syndicated loud mouth from San Francisco. Because of this, many young Canadians who want to work in radio are being denied what I enjoyed – the chance to find their voice and contribute to the fabric of Canadian communities.

Not to sound like a complete dinosaur, I acknowledge the harsh economic realities and understand that the first business of private radio is to stay in business. I've met some wonderful people from that part of the radio dial recently and know that, unlike the CBC, they are faced almost daily with the prospect of extinction. Furthermore, given the explosion of information sources over the past 25 years, I don't dispute that the role and relevancy of radio is changing.

But there is one profound truth about radio, regardless of all the modern pressures and forces brought to bear upon it. Whether it's the Saint John River overflowing its banks, or a blinding snowstorm in rural Quebec where I find myself now, there is nothing – nothing – to match that feeling of attachment to a community that only comes, like magic, through listening to local radio.

Another lesson that stuck from those days at CJCJ in Woodstock, New Brunswick, was that I learned not to say something about someone to the microphone that I wouldn't say to their face. This is about practicality, not superior etiquette.

In a small town, I would quite likely bump into that person somewhere later in the day. It forced me, if only for my physical well-being, to be civil and careful with words and opinions, and I never forgot to at least try, over the next 25 years, to present sometimes very difficult material in a way that was inoffensive and always inclusive. The media is full of people who want to use knowledge as a weapon and not a tool.

It seems a bit odd now that the memory of driving from Fredericton to Woodstock in 1971 to start that first paying job is still so crystal clear to me. I can even remember that it felt somehow appropriate when the Beatles' song *The Long and Winding Road* came on the radio as I took the Woodstock exit from the Trans-Canada Highway.

Alex Colville's painting "Seven Crows" is one of my favorites, and it always reminds me of that stretch of the Saint John River Valley between Fredericton and Woodstock. This ribbon of highway became, in the wee hours of the morning when radio signals are clearest, a place of dreams for me, and turning the radio on was like opening a box of treasures.

I'd discover gems like *The Owl's Nest* on WNEW from New York or hear how slick the guys were on WBZ from Boston. On the clearest nights, I might even catch rogue signals from Toronto and Montreal stations. I simply could not get enough and, like a sponge, soaked up technique, style, atmosphere, and in fact, anything and everything I thought might be useful someday.

You haven't lived until you've seen a full moon rise and spread like a heavenly flashlight across the land of the Saint John River valley. The golden light is caught for magical split-seconds by the water and reflected back at the stars which, to borrow the words of World War II correspondent Matthew Halton, twinkled like diamonds tossed across black velvet. And all the while, I drove along completely absorbed by the faraway dreams and possibilities promised by the radio dial.

I found the offices of CJCJ Radio on the second floor of a prominent building on Main Street, opposite the ubiquitous Maritime department store "Stedmans." You should know the characters.

I actually met station owner Bruce Groh once during Old Home week celebrations, when we broadcast from a trailer at the Fairgrounds. I'll never forget how hot it used to get in that trailer and how kids used to poke big globs of neon-colored cotton candy at us through the opened windows.

I saw station manager Bruce Smith, who hired me, just about every day. He had a great sense of humor and was full of stories about the history of the station. Dave Roberts was the program manager and "Goodtime" Charlie Russell juggled the accounting and the afternoon country music show.

There were more stories about the mysterious Walter than anyone else at the station. I never did meet him and only knew that he was a local farmer who had hosted the morning show and had once brought proceedings to a hilarious conclusion by asking Bruce Smith at a charity bowling tournament if he ever washed his "balls."

The two other disc jockeys in the early '70s at "CJ," as it was routinely called, became great friends and colleagues. Ray Landry, now one of the most successful and talented commercial voices in Canada, had replaced Walter as the morning man by the time I got there.

Ted "Chubby Buddy" Heyward is still in radio and is planning a move to the U.S. He did everything from news and commercials to Top 40 countdowns. Afternoons, evenings, weekends, holidays – when he wasn't drinking 12 litres of Coke and eating Hamburger Helper straight from the pot in the apartment he shared with Ray, Ted was at work.

I couldn't have asked for better people to begin a career with. As was almost everyone at the station, Ray and Ted were kind and funny and helpful and the three of us had a ball. Unlike President Clinton, we *did* inhale every now and then and one night it afforded us the chance to meet, unofficially, the police chief of Woodstock.

Before computers and compact discs, a radio station had to have a fairly large room where it could file all its albums. CJCJ's was at the front of the building with big windows facing Main Street. The room was a prime location from which to watch the Old Home Week parade each August.

During the rest of the year it was easy to hide out between the rows and rows of albums in the record library, especially after hours when the only threat was Rosie. Rosie cleaned the station and selected the music for a very popular daily religious half-hour show called *Four Leaf Clover*, which I hosted. Occasionally, she would barge through the studio door with her vacuum running full throttle while the microphone was wide open.

The rows between albums beckoned Ray and me early one evening and so with the building as quiet as a vault and with our pal Chubby on the air, we prepared for "take-off" in the library. We entered ever so silently and made sure the door was locked behind us – just in case.

We found a comfortable spot and weren't far along in our preparations when the light from the window was suddenly blocked by a figure standing at the end of our row. "Good evening," said the police chief, "how are you boys tonight?"

You can guess how "we boys" were. As we tried, ridiculously, to pretend we were doing something – anything – else, the chief explained that some of the parking meters along Main Street had been vandalized and how he too was hiding out to keep an eye on things for a couple of nights. Needless to say, his eyes weren't on us for very long as we beat a hasty retreat.

I had another brush with the chief one Saturday night when he called me at the station during my program to say he didn't know what was on the air but he had received complaints about the music I was playing. It was, as I recall, National Lampoon's wicked parody of the Woodstock music festival. Pretty funny stuff, but not for radio, at least not in Woodstock, New Brunswick. It was unusual that I never knew who bothered the chief with the complaints that night but, for the record, let me say this: you were right, and I promise I won't do it again.

Ray is easily one of the funniest people I've ever met and a very talented mimic. One of his specialties was the late actor Walter Brennan who you might remember had a pronounced limp. Ray's faultless impression incorporated this limp and that alone was guaranteed to crack me up.

Every day at noon I would play the scratchiest version you've ever heard of the *The Old Rugged Cross*, and then I would try to read, over this vinyl racket, the day's funeral announcements. This is how these announcements worked. The first sentence gave the name of the dearly departed. Then, I would bring the music up for ten seconds or so before finally reading the funeral arrangements and so on.

One day, just as the strains of *The Old Rugged Cross* began, I thought I saw out of the corner of my eye a split second flash of the dreaded Walter Brennan by the studio window. You have to understand just how helpless I was in the face of this impression. It could finish me off and leave me with tears of laughter running down my face anywhere, anytime and any place.

But not during funeral announcements. Surely, dear God, not during funeral announcements. I began to read the opening sentence and suddenly, I just knew *he* was there. I looked up praying and begging for a reprieve, but Walter had now come in full form before me and was limping across the studio window.

I managed to get the first sentence out naming the deceased and trusted I could get Ray to stop during the ten seconds while the music was up. He disappeared, I assumed because he saw the sheer terror in my eyes. As the music lowered and I began the few final sentences, not one but *two* Walters materialized in the window.

Unbelievably, Ray had been joined by station manager Bruce Smith and the two had formed an odd walking chorus line of Walters! I was told later that the end of the announcement sounded like I knew the deceased and had simply broken up having to read the notice of his death. I never said otherwise, and to this day, Ray can kill me with his Walter Brennan.

As much as I came to fear those funeral announcements at noon every day, I recognized that they were very much a part of the *real* service we provided. They acted as a means of staying in touch for everyone in the community but, also, they never let us, as broadcasters, forget who we were talking to and what mattered in that community.

We were never allowed to stray very far from our roots in a small New Brunswick town, as I had learned the night of the National Lampoon parody episode. The "voice" of CJCJ was very much of that time and place, and the effort to reflect the values and concerns of the surrounding area meant the station sold considerable air time to religious groups.

Programs like *Back to the Bible* were staples for us and it was my job each evening to make sure everything went smoothly. We even had live programs featuring the ministers and members of local congregations who'd come in and raise the roof with their preaching and singing.

It was truly community radio and I remember all of it, especially the feeling of belonging, with great fondness.

THREE

GOING PUBLIC

I can't remember why I wanted to work for the Canadian Broad-casting Corporation. It certainly wasn't from any sense of loy-alty or familiarity since I grew up in a household where CBC radio and television were practically non-existent. I had clearly fallen in love with radio, but my need for a job after finishing university was greater than any commitment I felt at that time to public broadcasting.

A curious thing about CBC radio back then – it sounded better and seemed to mean more outside Toronto. It's still true to some extent, but in the early '70s in Fredericton, there was only one other awful choice on the dial, and as a friend of mine is fond of saying, that choice "could make your ears bleed." So aside from CHSR, which was really only available on the cam-pus of the University of New Brunswick, the CBC was it.

In addition, I loved Fredericton and although I'd gone there four years before, knowing nothing about the Maritimes and fully expecting to return to Montreal, I now couldn't imagine leaving New Brunswick. I suppose that sounds a bit like nostalgic comfort food but, you know, it isn't only a product of time and memory.

I was aware *then* that these were very special and wonderful years and I shared them with the love of my life and a bunch of cats in a beautiful house along the Saint John River. I don't know that I've ever been happier in that smooth and uncomplicated way that seems to bless youth.

I met a young woman recently who was just starting out professionally and she told me that to get ahead, she had changed jobs eight times in the past two and a half years. She's smart, good at her work, and knows what she wants, so having to jump through hoop after hoop is not a reflection on her abilities. But she seemed unsure that she'd ever get what she wanted from her work.

I'm reminded by such experiences of how lucky I was to have had a career that, for the most part, directed itself. I never really know quite what to answer when asked by a young person about how to start out in journalism these days. Until recently, I never planned any move and the truth is, it wasn't until I lost it that it even felt like a "career."

But I did always know that the wheelbarrow full of opportunities presented to me was bigger than any skill or quality I may have possessed as a broadcaster. That's not false modesty. There always seemed to be something else for me to go on to with a new set of challenges and possibilities.

With good, smart young people struggling to get a footing these days, I feel a bit sheepish about the relative ease I enjoyed in 25 years of making a living through broadcasting. I was proud to be part of an organization which not only knew what it was about, but acted in ways that understood and respected its mandate as the *public* broadcaster of Canada.

I was able to just kind of fall into the next thing that grabbed my attention. Anyone who has worked in the media long enough understands that one of the richest dividends of the business is the challenge of constant change. In addition to not only saving but making the world a better place for all living creatures, journalists have a shorter attention span than a hummingbird at a dry feeder.

We can last about a maximum of two minutes before turning the conversation back to our own fascinating lives. I'm guilty on all counts and even now, while I return to my "fascinating life" – these are *my* memoirs after all – I think I now recognize a consequence, with perhaps some importance, of having had it so easy professionally.

Precisely because I never had to sit down and worry and plot and plan the next move, I never really learned how to, or wanted to, make a distinction between my working and my personal life. This is a fine path to follow, as long as everything stays on the rails.

It's always been wise advice – and I gave it to others many times – not to allow one's work to define one's value and self-esteem in life. But that's much easier said than done. I admit I could never do it and, as a result, my work was very much the foundation of my life. I think I depended on it for too much.

That, dear reader, is a very awkward confession for me because I had always hoped to be smarter than to place so much of my self-esteem in the hands of, essentially, strangers. It is a hard lesson to learn that work alone will not lead to a full life and it is a lesson I suspect is best learned privately.

But allow me just a few words on the subject, if only because I'd like some company. I know I'm not alone struggling with the role work plays in my life. For all of us who have done essentially the same thing now since we joined the workforce 25 years ago or so, the words of Matthew Fox from his book *The Reinvention of Work* ring true.

He's careful to make the distinction between working for a living and "being worked" for a living. It's only natural that our expectations from work should change along with our lives, but it's not easy to carve yourself a new niche or level of endeavor.

Fox quotes Thomas Aquinas', "The objects of the heart are truth and justice," and goes on to write, "Our work must make way for the heart, that is, for truth and justice to play an ever increasing role in our professional lives. Without that heart-food," he concludes, "we will surely die of starvation of the spirit, and all the promotions and fat paychecks in the world will not assuage the feeling that we are dying in the soul."

I'm coming to understand only now how there were really two elements at play which made my departure from the CBC so personally wrenching. One had to do with the cracking of that personal foundation which I had allowed my work to give me through the years, and second, the work itself was drifting further and further from the search for justice and truth.

Undoubtedly, my needs were changing, so it's also possible that the level of commitment I wanted from the job was unrealistic. But in any case, I believed to an unhealthy extent that I *was* what I *did*. Of course, the media is the porch light for moths like me and a perfect haven for all the "shy egomaniacs." Even with moderate success, it can be a very seductive world with its offers of celebrity and money.

Even the relatively scant public attention I had caused me trouble and left me feeling increasingly trapped. It's not one of those juicy *People* magazine stories of redemption, but in my own way, I worried that the values which had come to mean the most to me and to inform my life were becoming distorted and twisted out of shape. It might help you to know here that I am to worrying what McDonald's is to fast food hamburgers. But it doesn't make the worrying any less real.

Whatever was happening to that centre we all have where values rest, I was the one who let it happen. I remember as a kid, after a heavy rain, finding a popsicle stick and tossing it in the water rushing to the drain at the end of our street. As a professional, I felt like that stick at times, rushing forward with no sense of where I was heading or control over the path I took.

I absolutely loved the attention at first and the pursuit of it gave me the energy to work ridiculously long hours. I allowed it, at some personal cost, to consume just about every waking moment of my life. But as I got older and valued privacy more while the media generally seemed to value it less, I found that kind of attention a little unsettling.

When I was working on the television program *Midday*, the senior producer Susanne Boyce ordered me to take a week off and to go away. A few days later, I found myself sitting in a restaurant in Mexico. A very polite man came over to the table and said, "My wife and I are having this discussion and we're sure you're somebody?" Proof that a celebrity is somebody who is famous for being well known.

It certainly hasn't been easy for me or very pleasant for those around me, but I have discovered, in this process of clearing out the rubble of that old work foundation, a promising site from which to build a new life.

This sort of stuff, I've learned, means nothing until you're ready for it and I'm as skeptical as you may be about many of the formulas and strategies flogged shamelessly by those in the so-called human potential movement.

All I can tell you at this point is that whatever it is that's happening within me it is very real, and it feels so much closer to my heart that I'm increasingly coming to trust and embrace it with enthusiasm. When you confuse your job with your self, life becomes little more than just another mindless task, with practically no joy or wonder. I started with plenty of both at CBC in Fredericton.

Ray DeBoer was the station manager and Leon Cole was the P.O.O., an unfortunate acronym for the program operations officer, one eagerly used as an adjective by non-listeners. Here's the kind of place it was.

On weekends I would sometimes go to the station, which had a darkroom in the basement, and Ray would show me how to develop black and white film. I recall the first time in there with him. Just as he was developing something, I lit a cigarette. I'm sure he wanted to, but didn't return the firing.

Leon Cole went on to be a very successful and talented broadcaster as host of the CBC radio program *R.S.V.P.*, but he now finds himself, proudly I'm sure, in the position of being better known as jazz singer Holly Cole's father.

A few years ago, Leon was broadcasting his program live from the atrium in that colossal tomb that houses what's left of the CBC on Front Street in Toronto when I happened to walk by. He energetically grabbed me and proudly announced to his live audience assembled there that he, Leon Cole, was the one who first hired Peter Downie at the corporation.

Poor, dear Leon. Poor, dear me. There was almost no reaction, virtually none. There was a smattering of "Who?" and "What did he say?"

As I quickly tried to make my getaway from the embarrassing silence descending upon the atrium, a lovely older woman came over. We talked for a bit until she said she knew my father when he was the minister of some church or other.

I responded politely that she must have me confused with someone else because my father was (a) dead, and (b) never a minister. She looked quite startled and asked, "Aren't you Peter Togni?" At the time, Togni hosted *Stereo Morning* on CBC radio.

I've told Leon that I couldn't imagine spending my first days at the CBC with anyone better. He brought to the job a contagious sense of humor and passion for the work which remain with me to this day. How lucky I was to cut my CBC teeth with Leon Cole.

I can never repay him adequately for his early encouragement and patience, both professionally and personally. He and manager Ray DeBoer introduced me to public broadcasting in a way that was to stay with me until the end of my career with the CBC. And I must face the truth that it has ended. But there is still so much I want to communicate and accomplish that I'm hopeful of finding a new way to stay in touch.

The continuing dreadful cuts in funding have been clearly damaging to the corporation, but they've also been used to cover inept and visionless management. The cry of "no money" is the new mantra of the creatively bankrupt. The CBC is going through a Near *Life* Experience – no bright white light reported or needed, as the bland lead the bland.

I was one who acquired the taste for public broadcasting as I grew older and I still remember the excitement I felt in joining the corporation. That feeling was due to much more than the relief that came with finally getting a decent paycheque. It was the promise of being part of an extended electronic family which not only welcomed, but encouraged diversity.

Anyone could walk through the door and fight to have a piece put on the radio with programs like *Five Nights*, *Between Ourselves*, *Identities*, or *Concern*. The difference between then and now is not money, but attitude. It was then a directed and vibrant organization where the air was electric with possibility and creativity.

The pursuit of excellence guided those of us who took great pride in calling ourselves public broadcasters. As a new public broadcaster, I learned from listening to Max Ferguson and Allan McFee. And I drew on the emotional attachment I came to feel with *This Country in the Morning* and to Peter Gzowski.

It was Gzowski, in particular, who had the single greatest impact on me as a broadcaster. When I was about to meet and interview him for the first time, shortly after my arrival at the CBC in Fredericton, my nerves prevented me from sleeping for two nights. Like a golf pro who can play thousands of rounds of golf but still tell you in minute detail the lovely shot made 15 years ago at Pebble Beach, I can remember almost every part of that first conversation I had with Peter.

My innocence surprises even me as I recall the end of that interview. I told him *on air*, that I hadn't been sleeping well, awaiting his arrival, because he did what he did so well and it was what I wanted to do for a living. I cringe remembering that now, but not for the reason you might think.

It's not so much that I am, in fact, a little embarrassed to tell you of my naiveté, but I ache for the poor audience in Fredericton, which had foisted upon it surely more than it ever wanted to know about me and my dreams – not to mention how poor Peter felt about it all.

He was, understandably, taken aback by my public declaration of admiration and, in return, chose or felt compelled to say something nice about my honesty and career prospects. He wrote four words in the back of his book which meant the world to me. He scribbled, "You're on your way." I suspect he would be supremely uncomfortable to know that that book with its dedication still holds a place of distinction in my home and warmth in my heart. I'll consider it progress not to cringe at those words in another 25 years!

Shortly after our meeting in Fredericton, Peter was in Calgary and generously mentioned my name, in a speech, as a broadcaster to watch for. My sister, in the audience that day, is still not over her shock.

I also recall many nights, sitting in my car by the Saint John River, absorbing the world as it was told to me by Barbara Frum. I'll never forget that almost contagious pride as a Canadian bubbling to the surface, listening to her brilliance.

Even though I was hundreds of miles from them and tucked away in the relative obscurity of New Brunswick, Gzowski and Frum convinced me every day on the radio that, as public broadcasters, we were there to offer something different.

It was a given that there would always be a larger audience elsewhere. It didn't matter to us – not because we didn't care, but precisely because we took great pride remaining true to that group of Canadians who wanted something unique from its public broadcaster.

In an almost total victory of short-sightedness driven by audience relations types and directed by budget crunchers and market forces, the CBC now seems to be in a mad rush to be like everybody else. But like the poor kid chosen last for the pickup team at the hockey rink, the one who lacks the skill but loves the game, the CBC is left to sadly tug for attention at the pant leg of public opinion in a game it hardly knows.

One of the wonderful results of my 25 years of broadcasting is that whether it's the airstrip at Tuktoyaktuk, a hotel in Campbell River, a gas station in Edmunston, or the Town Hall in Portugal Cove, I'm likely to meet someone who just wants to say hi or to remind me of an interview or part of a program which I had completely forgotten. And to think it all began with vanilla ice cream.

Leon Cole's first task of many in our relationship was to grade my dreaded CBC announcer's test when I applied for the position of announcer/operator in Fredericton.

I sat in the padded opulence of a CBC studio to face page after page of names of classical composers, words and phrases that looked to me like severely vowel-challenged mumbo jumbo. You have to keep in mind that for me at this time, Alvin Lee's rendition of *Going Home* with *Ten Years After* at Woodstock was the definition of a classic.

I went on to prove this categorically soon after by announcing that an upcoming CBC program would feature the compositions of "Wratch-minoff," in place of Rachmaninoff. Come to think of it, Alvin Lee's performance still rates as a classic.

There was an ad lib part of the test which gave me a multiple choice of topics. I don't recall the choices, only that my topic was my favorite ice cream and I stumbled, hemmed, and hawed my way through the next two minutes. My career as a public broadcaster was launched by a short and pathetic essay on the joys of vanilla ice cream.

Twenty five years later, my finely honed intuition tells me that fudge ripple would at least have been a richer source of material. Somehow, in spite of the test, I got the job.

One of the things I had to learn very early on was to talk to time. In other words, if I had a 30-second break, 26 seconds didn't cut it. It becomes – forgive the pun – second nature. But at first, I was terrified to go too long or to come up short.

One of my first station breaks, as they're called, was to announce a classical concert in honor of the Easter season.

This was a time, you might remember, when it was believed that the local stations along the network would enjoy a stronger local identification by using their own call letters. For example, Montreal CBC was called CBM, Ottawa was CBO and so on.

In New Brunswick at the time, CBC Fredericton programmed CBC in Saint John. So I would read the designated announcement for 23 seconds, pause, close the key to Saint John and then, using the local call letters for the Fredericton station, announce, "This is CBZ in Fredericton."

I would then calmly close that key, open the one to Saint John and, remembering their call letters, say "This is CBD in Saint John." The veterans might even say, "You're *listening* to CBD in Saint John," but I wasn't yet ready for that kind of intricate verbal gymnastic.

After identifying the so-called "local" stations in Saint John and Fredericton so everyone knew exactly what they were listening to, my next task was to open both keys and give the assembled multitudes the time check just before the news. I had done this a million times in my sleep. I was ready. Show me to the microphone.

You don't know what nervous is until you've launched into a 30-second break with no feeling for the time, fully aware that if you went too long, the unforgiving Master Computer located somewhere along this vast, elaborate, electronic Maginot Line, charged with the national defence of all that was good and proper about public broadcasting, would cut you off like a power failure and then crush you with the entire weight of The Network as it steamrollered your little announcement and your job. The whole shebang was in my hands as I prepared to take my place on the front lines.

I can almost remember the script verbatim. I cleared my throat, coaxing my CBC voice and timidly began.

"In honor of the Easter season, CBC radio proudly celebrates this most solemn Christian occasion tonight, by presenting Dryden's *Hum Roll Mass*."

I knew immediately that something was wrong and realized to my utter horror, frantically scanning the page before me, that it was in fact "*Haydn's Drum Roll Mass*."

"Don't panic, oh my God, I've blown it, don't panic, I'll never work again, just don't panic, how long is this taking? Don't panic, the entire network is waiting for me to finish, stay calm, with no money the cats won't be able to eat, try to control your breathing, what if I don't work, take your time, curse those classical composers, and Ken Dryden for that matter, take your time!"

I tried to get a grip, paused as any smooth professional might, offered my apologies, and then repeated, "That's Dryden's *Hum Roll Mass*."

By now, it had to be time for the station IDs, I screamed at myself. But I was so profoundly flustered, I probably couldn't even have told you my name. Of course, the longer this disaster continued, the more a nameless kind of anonymity seemed attractive.

This is where the "operator" part of "announcer/operator" becomes fairly crucial. With the steady hands of a surgeon I missed both station keys on the board, leaving the two cities wide open for my next announcement: "You're listening to CBDead."

And you thought I was fooling about Leon Cole's patience.

There was another occasion when time caused me grief, when CBC radio still ran commercials. This little escapade started when four of us went to a drive-in movie on a Sunday night and proceeded to devour some "special" brownies, made by the other couple. I include that information not to escape responsibility, but only to say I had no idea how powerful these brownies were.

They turned out to be special alright, so extraordinary that they were still with me the next morning when I started to read a 60-second commercial during one of the scheduled breaks in *This Country in the Morning*.

After reading a Rambler commercial for what seemed like hours and with the *Hum Roll Mass* memory still fresh, I bailed out, convinced I had gone way too long. There were 47 seconds of silence remaining before network programming kicked in again. I went to Leon, said I wasn't well and went home.

The Fredericton Press Club was just beginning in the early '70s and it was a centre of activity, as I recall, most Friday nights. We used to gather there to wonder where Patty Hearst was (we concluded that CBC publicity had to be handling her, as no one had a clue where she was) and to listen to Bill Akerley sing *Brazil* as he launched another noisy attack in our weekly game of Risk®. Press Clubs are a good idea. Everyone recognizes the neurosis of those around them and all unwind by typically drinking away another week that was.

I remember one night sitting upstairs when this fellow literally plopped down in the couch across from me, sending half the beer from his glass spiraling upwards in a mini-twister, which then splashed all over him. I was quite surprised that he didn't seem to mind the mess and even more surprised to recognize the premier of the province, Richard Hatfield.

There have been few people I enjoyed speaking with or spending time with more than the late Richard Hatfield. If you ever listened in on any of those seemingly endless federal/provincial conferences at which he was always such a colorful participant, you know he was rarely a man of few words.

But I remember once during a radio show, reaching him by phone at his home in Hartland on his birthday, when he was completely flummoxed by my question. I can still hear him stammering and stuttering his way to a most uncharacteristic silence. You know what question did him in?

"So what did you get for your birthday?"

The next time we met at some function, I asked him why he had trouble answering such a simple question. He said he'd never expected to be asked about his birthday presents and had frozen in a way that had only come over him once before.

Richard Hatfield was a gifted storyteller. He had us in stitches as he remembered that other time he had frozen, leaving the New Brunswick Legislature one afternoon only to be confronted on the steps by a woman protester with a baby in her arms.

The screaming, distraught woman held out the baby and Hatfield said at one point he was absolutely certain that she was going to make her point by spiking the baby on the steps, like a player in the NFL does with the football after a touchdown. He played a wonderfully horrified observer.

I always found the snickering and kind of nudge-nudge quality of the gossip surrounding his personal life to be not just silly, but mean-spirited. And although I don't pretend to have known him well at all, I think I can say that mean-spirited was not one of his qualities.

Whether you agreed with his view or not, he always brought a passion to his politics and a conviction to the stands he took on various public issues. Yes, he wore his heart on his sleeve, but as Winston Churchill might say, "Some heart. Some sleeve." I think Canada is a poorer place for his absence.

His predecessor actually gave me quite a start one day as I was lining up interviews for the afternoon radio show I was doing in Fredericton. I expected that I would just leave a message for Louis Robichaud to call me back.

You could have knocked me off the chair with a fiddlehead when he actually answered the phone at his house. I guess we all take turns at stammering and stuttering and although the former premier was gracious about my call, I'm sure he was confused by my own unusual bout of silence.

There's a real skill in lining up and arranging interviews. I am not good at it. It feels like a meal before a meal to me. I enjoy the energy that comes with a fresh conversation and if I've already spoken to you on the phone about the content of the interview, it feels a bit wilted to me once we're on air.

There are masters at this job and I had the great pleasure of working with and receiving credit for the superb work of talented producers at CBC programs like *As It Happens* and

Morningside. More than hosts want to admit, the really good producers also know how to transfer a sense of confidence.

The best I've ever met is my dear friend Gary Katz, but Marlene McArdle, now with CTV, and Anne Bayin, now in a senior position with Pamela Wallin, are also terrific producers. I still remember Anne lining up a ballet choreographer for me to interview once and, aware of my nervousness and my cultural blind spot, she reassured me that it was very similar to a quarterback arranging a play on the field.

Of course, it isn't at all but her wise advice worked. My knees stopped knocking long enough for me to welcome the guest.

Good producers are the reason a program succeeds. Bad producers are the reason scotch was invented. Producers, good and bad, are generally the ones who have the most to do with the naming of a program, if only because they have to call a million times a day and identify themselves as being with such and such a show.

Most producers don't share Terry Gilliam's sense of humor. This former Monty Python-er told us on *Midday* that he named his production company something like "Poo-Poo Productions" only because he wanted to force high-powered, snooty attorneys in three-piece suits, seated around a mahogany conference table, to have to say "Poo-Poo Productions."

In fact, once struggling against the deadline to come up with a program name, we all sat exhausted, indifferently tossing out suggestions. Dismissing one of them, somebody said, "I refuse to get Dick Cavett on the phone to say, 'I'm calling from such and such a show in Canada.'"

We were all so tired at that point of trying to choose a name acceptable to everyone that the CBC Stereo network came dangerously close to having a show called "Hello, Dick?" Has a certain panache, don't you think?

In Fredericton, I was on my own – no technician to handle the board and no producer to line up guests. Occasionally, it got me into trouble. Every afternoon, I'd talk to the weather man at about 5:25, if I remember correctly.

This one day, everything and then some had hit the fan and I only had seconds to dial the weather office and scream, "I'll be right with you." I would then put the call through the board and go on air with the forecast.

I was so tight for time as the record was ending that I clipped his response and only heard a bit of what sounded like "Sure," before putting him on the program.

"So, time now for our regular weather report. So-and-so's on the line from the weather office. Hi there," I said as always.

There was an unusual and unexpected pause and my first thought was I must have made a mistake patching the call through, but then the weather man cleared his throat and replied, "What, are you calling from a radio station or something?"

That afternoon, we heard what the weather was like at this poor fellow's house, whose number I had mistakenly dialed. There's a similar story that makes the rounds of someone calling for Rich Little at a hotel and ending up with Little Richard on the air. If it isn't true, it should be.

When I think back to the time in Fredericton, I realize how much I laughed on the job. I remember in particular an incident involving the morning news reader Bob Richards in a similar situation.

Bob had one of those great authoritative voices which made everything he said, from ordering a coffee to announcing disasters, sound completely credible. Except this one time: "Good morning, I'm Bob Richards with the CBC 6 a.m. news. In the headlines, the prime minister's moth is dead."

Pierre Trudeau's mother had passed away overnight and the typewriter in the newsroom simply left off the "er." Bob was reminded to have a glance at the script before launching into the newscast.

Legend also has it that one morning, after going through the line-up of that day, the host said, "But first with the news, is Bob Richards," and Bob began as he did every single day, "Good morning, in the headlines...," looked down and realized he had forgotten the newscast in the newsroom.

It's amazing that anyone sounds even remotely awake, let alone lucid at 6 a.m., but the ridiculous, punishing hours required to do morning radio are precisely what builds a real and unique team feeling that makes it such a special time period to fill.

But I had my hands full at the other end of the day with the afternoon show. I remember a limerick contest based on Malcolm Bricklin's ill-fated business venture. I will never forget listening to the eminent Walter Learning from Theatre New Brunswick, and later of the Canada Council, as he took part in a gargling contest over the phone. And try as I might, I can't forget being subpoenaed as the only man to attend a private dinner with Margaret Atwood and a group of feminists hell-bent on educating me.

Betty Soutter was like a mother to all of us who worked at CBC in Fredericton and although I remember everyone I worked with there, she stands out.

I also recall actually having a life in Fredericton. Summer weekends were spent rafting with those "brownie" friends on a river ten minutes from home, or languishing on the beaches of P.E.I., with the only worry being the choice between lobster or clams for dinner.

I volunteered for a time at the local S.P.C.A., but after being called out to rescue a badly injured cat one night, only to have him die in my care as we waited for the vet clinic to open, I knew I just didn't have the emotional detachment that enables a person to function in that kind of work.

I thought of that very cat as I stood in a refugee camp in southern Bangladesh years later.

Thousands of Muslims had fled persecution in their native Myonmar and were now crammed in these tents in the southernmost tip of Bangladesh with insufferable heat matched by stubborn disease. As I stood in the middle of one tent trying to digest what lay before me, I felt the tiniest bump imaginable on my foot.

I looked down to discover this poor, impossibly thin kitten whose clouded eyes and crippled body begged for an end. I gently took this little heartbeat in my hands, left the tent just to get away, and proceeded to cry my eyes out. With the help of a volunteer nurse from Nova Scotia, we managed to brush a little milk across the lips of this poor creature, but it was way too little and way too late. I hadn't realized the endurance of that Fredericton memory until that day so many years later in Bangladesh.

There were other lessons from Fredericton which remain with me to this day. When Malcolm Bricklin's sports car misadventure finally ended and all the limericks had been collected and read on my program *Fresh Air*, I reached then-provincial Liberal leader Robert Higgins, who was going to judge the winners. He had gone along with the contest through all the stages of the odd Bricklin/Hatfield waltz, but on this afternoon, he couldn't play along.

He explained that it was a difficult day for those who had just lost their jobs and although he understood the nature of the contest, he didn't want to appear to find anything funny about that situation. It seems a bit odd to me that I remember that so clearly after all this time, but it obviously said something that stuck with me about public integrity and honor.

A professor of psychology at the University of New Brunswick, whose name I wish I remembered, stopped me cold in my tracks one winter when I was trying to get him to come on the program to talk about the strategies and tricks used by advertisers at Christmas.

His impassioned denunciation of the use of children in advertising and the detrimental impact on them by this steady and relentless commercial barrage was years ahead of its time and planted the seeds of social morality and responsibility in my approach to practicing journalism.

I also learned an important lesson about the role of the CBC. As you might remember, there was a time in this country when Prime Minister Pierre Trudeau and the premiers would gather in these elaborately staged federal/provincial conferences and CBC radio would provide live coverage.

They would most often run long – many times, as a matter of fact, due to Hatfield – and the afternoon show I was hosting would start late.

One day, I began by offering a mild, tongue-in-cheek complaint about the length of the conference just ended. Later, someone called to say how important the CBC was in being the only source of coverage of events like this and that I should value the station for providing the service no one else would. She was right and so was the CBC back then.

A quick calculation tells me I have moved nine times since leaving Fredericton in 1976 and I still lug around with me boxes of letters and program logs from those days. It occurs to me that if the survival of memory over distance and time is an indication of value and worth, then my life was clearly enriched by having worked in that building on the hill in Fredericton. It is a time worth remembering and I'm grateful for having had the chance to meet and work with such good and kind people.

FOUR

LIFE IN THE ME-DIA

I'm asked sometimes whether I preferred working in television over radio. There's no short answer, as each medium has its own distinctive set of challenges, rewards and frustrations. But, mercifully, there is no American public radio network the size of the CBC and so Canadian radio is not led by people who'd rather be in New York or Los Angeles.

To be sure, some network radio managers deserve to be shipped to their own private wilderness, but to radio's credit, it is generally accepted that being Canadian does not mean being inferior. I heard again and again, during my time at *Man Alive*, for example, comments like "Canadians are such lousy talkers," or "Canadians don't look good on TV." It would be amusing, if it weren't so sad.

So my answer to the question of radio or television in my days at the CBC generally comes down on the side of radio. Although I think there are signs of real trouble brewing there, it has some way to go before reaching the sell-out level of CBC television.

And the bar of excellence in radio was set so high so early on in my career that it will remain a challenge for the rest of my life to even come close to that mark.

In the grand scheme of things, the summer of 1976, when that bar was set, came about five years too early for me. In a personal sense, I wasn't ready for it all at the age of 25. Professionally, it was a creative and vibrant experience that I never wanted to end.

In the mid-'70s, CBC regional radio was alive and healthy with many excellent people deciding to pursue a career in Halifax or Calgary or Yellowknife. Unfortunately, I was cursed with a different kind of ambition which pointed me in the direction of the network in Toronto.

When I first started to work for the CBC in Fredericton and wondered where I would go from there, I had in the back of my mind that I would like to do a program on the network by the time I was 30. But as it happened, I left Fredericton quite quickly when my personal life headed south and I ended up in Toronto working as a producer with Peter Gzowski on a program aptly titled *Gzowski on FM*.

This was on the then newly launched stereo network of CBC radio. I think the essential idea behind *Gzowski on FM* was to keep Peter busy and off the streets until his television show was ready to go.

In the end, it didn't only keep *him* busy. As a producer, I gave new meaning to the adjective "undistinguished." The role of a producer on a show like this one is first, to make sure the guest shows up, and second, to make sure the host is well-armed with information and tips on what that guest is going to say. I presented Peter with the grand total of one item in three months, and even on that one outstanding occasion he had started the interview by the time I raced to the studio with the research material and background.

But at least I got to witness and learn from one of the best. Once, when I was going to be sitting in for him as host, I was busy editing a pre-recorded interview I had done with the Quebec actress Denise Pelletier. I was working on it in the main area of the *Gzowski on FM* office and he overheard a question-and-answer sequence. As he walked by to leave for that day, he sneaked me a note which, when uncrinkled, read, "Don't ask questions that can be answered yes or no." I took it to mean we were friends.

Singer Dan Hill and I had a conversation about mentors light years ago when we were both starting out and comparing notes. Dan told me how awkward he felt, at first, around the already accomplished singer/songwriter Murray MacLaughlin. I had similar moments of discomfort around Gzowski and was relieved when Dan explained how one game of baseball with MacLaughlin had erased the problem. Regrettably, Gzowski and I never found the equivalent of that baseball game and we went on to perfect a kind of strange "un"-relationship over the years.

Think of the most competitive person in your life, multiply by ten, and you'd have about a quarter of Peter Gzowski's drive. The combination of our ambitions, his mistaken conviction that I was after his job, and mutual degrees of shyness probably prevented us from developing a more solid friendship. But, having said that, he has never been anything but straight with me – which sometimes I have resented – and generous toward me professionally, and I will always be grateful for his guidance and example.

I would also jump at the chance, asking no questions, if the opportunity arose again to work with skilled producers like Anne Bayin or Gary Katz, both of whom were with Gzowski before me.

I now think of this two-hour radio program as the quintessential example of what public broadcasting could be in Canada. First, and this needs to be said given what's happening today, it was unabashedly Canadian and second, it was a daily, joyful celebration of *our* music, poetry, writing, painting, comedy and other artistic endeavors. It was a live two hours every weekday afternoon and I just drank it all in.

We also just drank, sometimes, usually at a place called The Red Lion across from the CBC building on Jarvis Street. One afternoon a kind of vision appeared on Jarvis Street. This was before the beer, I hasten to add. It was a typical hot and humid afternoon in Toronto and this figure in a white suit, kind of shimmering around the edges like a dream, weaved his way along the sidewalk and let out a grunt of recognition when he saw Gzowski at our table. It was my first and last meeting with the late reporter Norman DePoe.

Another afternoon, a bunch of us, including Gzowski and the poet Susan Musgrave, gathered around the picnic tables provided outdoors for our usual dunking in draft beer.

I think Susan and I took an almost instant dislike to each other without even so much as a word being exchanged between us. I have no idea why, and thanks to too many beers, I can't recall specifically what I said about poetry or the appearance of poets on the program. But I do distinctly remember her turning to Peter and saying, "See, I told you."

I never, ever expected that when Peter left I would be asked to host the new show, and the remark Susan made was the kind which would have me up sweating at three in the morning wondering if I was a fraud. Luckily, I was so busy I couldn't sit and get an ulcer over it. There would be plenty of time for that in the future.

The show which followed *Gzowski on FM* was called *The Entertainment Section*. This is the program which came dangerously close to being named *Hello, Dick?* After our futile attempts to pick a name, it was Gzowski with his newspaper roots who suggested *The Entertainment Section*. Done. Now what do we do?

What the producers did was hold my hand, line up great guests, and put together, day in and day out, a challenging, lively and interesting two hours. Please forgive the boasting, but minus my obvious inexperience, I would hold up *The Entertainment Section* and defy anyone to put a better radio program on the air.

What *I* did, while the producers were busy with all of that, was smoke like a chimney and try desperately to keep my head above water. There's an invigoration which comes from such daily proximity to death. That explains why I have never enjoyed myself more than I did during those packed and terrifying days of *The Entertainment Section*.

In some ways, they reminded me of when I was a youngster, practically living on the outdoor rinks of Montreal playing hockey until my legs felt like noodles. Once a bunch of big, older guys – they were probably 17 or even 18 years old – came on the rink and I was faced with the choice of staying and playing with them or leaving.

I still remember Bob Berry, who went on to coach in the NHL, convincing me to play by saying the only way to get better was to play with those who had more experience. *The Entertainment Section* felt like that.

But I now understand age is not the only factor determining those who become buffeted by celebrity. Even now, when the excuse of youth is gone, I'm still made extremely uncomfortable by recognition, and this, I think, is at the centre of my unease with what I did for a living for so long. I never quite learned to treat it as a game.

Just before I left the CBC, a story about me showed up in something called *The Radio Guide*. The interview was done over the phone by someone in Vancouver just before I left for Prince Edward Island. It was a dreadful interview and my fault. As I lay on the beach that summer, I thought I'd have to call that reporter when I got home to see if we could try it again.

When I reached her, she agreed it had been awful and said it sounded to her editor as if I wasn't proud of anything I had done at the CBC. It was a comment which stunned me and forced me to realize that I couldn't pretend much longer, that if I sounded that way to a stranger, maybe I had to examine what I was doing.

The reporter and I tried again, and once again, I found myself stumbling over the subject of my personal involvement in the stories I had covered. To say it would have been easier not to get involved seemed ridiculous to me and wasn't how I felt. Nevertheless, I heard words like that coming from my mouth. I think I know now what I was trying to say.

It wasn't that I was too personally involved in the work I did. It was that the wrong part of me was too involved. I've learned that there is a heavy price to be paid when you allow others to define your life.

I wouldn't trade any of it for the world, but on most days now, I am happy that I got out. Clearly, I needed some time away from it to gain a little perspective – not so much on the business, as on myself. I'm not sure if I'll ever do that kind of work again. I am sure, however, that I want to spend more time seeking paths that make sense to my heart and soul.

I spoke with my friend Sue Prestedge recently and we laughed at how what had seemed important to us at one stage of our lives, now wasn't. And we wondered how we ever had the energy for the kind of daily television we once did together. Sue and her husband, Tim McKenna, a tremendously gifted photographer/journalist in Toronto, are rare examples of those in the media who are well-grounded. And I think it's reflected in the solid and honest work of each of them.

Maybe the question of energy was on my mind when I spoke with Sue on the phone because it seems to be one of the better words to describe that incredible summer of '76. It was a time of great passion and intensity in my life.

The decision was made that before I replaced Peter, I should make a few appearances as a "columnist," to help introduce myself to the national audience. The most memorable appearance had to do with the traditional fireworks displays around the long Victoria Day weekend.

I was sent, with a producer and a technician whose names I'll leave out in case they're still at it, to the Hand Chemical Company outside Toronto to describe the scene as they set off over $2000 worth of fireworks. Just for us.

The idea was that I would then take this edited tape of booms and bangs and *oohs* and *aahhhs* to the studio to have a talk with Peter. Well, when we got back to the office we discovered that the tape machine had, in fact, not been put in the "record" mode. One result, at the moment of this discovery, was that we had plenty of booms and bangs in the office. Just nothing on tape. Somebody – eyes darting around the room here – had to tell the Hand Chemical Company. It wasn't me.

I had my own problems with the deafening silence on that tape. I think the segment with Peter the next afternoon was scheduled for about 15 minutes and, without any tape, that's lots of talk about fireworks. More than I had certainly, but it taught me a lesson about acting on radio.

As Peter and I were walking down the hallway toward the studio the next day, he asked how much one could conceivably spend on a private fireworks display. I told him and he kind of just grunted. I was amazed how new the figure seemed to be to him on air and how much more interested he seemed to be then than moments before.

Whatever else is said of Peter's time at *Morningside*, it was his ability to still sound interested which I find most worthy of congratulations. There are only so many limericks and fudge recipes in the world and I'm sure he's heard them all twice over by now. There had to be mornings when he wanted to scream, but I think he was always saved, as I have been, by the imagination, loyalty and caring of the CBC radio audience.

It may strike you as odd that we would even have *tried* to put a fireworks display on the radio, but we were always tackling things like that. I recall one afternoon when Peter had this traveling circus visiting, with really only his commentary to describe the color and action. Clown shoes and polka dot pants don't make a lot of noise.

You have to know a bit of the geography here. There was a kind of secondary hallway outside the control room which led to the studio. I went barging through on this occasion, not knowing that a unicyclist was balancing against the inside of the door, using the corridor to pick up speed for some stunt in the main studio.

Peter was running out of words, and assorted circus characters in big shoes and bright costumes were lying on the floor, breathlessly waiting for the unicyclist to fly up the ramp and over them "with the greatest of ease." Despite Peter's announcement and cue that all was ready, it was evident that something had gone horribly wrong in the corridor.

As I frantically scraped the now shocked and swearing unicyclist off the wall, I believe that off in the distance that afternoon on radio, far behind Peter's increasingly expectant commentary, you may have heard a muffled, "Here, let me help you get back up." In my own small way, I guess I was introducing myself to the audience. We don't seem to have events like that – or me, for that matter – on the radio anymore.

We had a contest that summer where well-known people would be invited to tell us the details of a classic story in three minutes, one which they could choose from a list of three options they were given live on air. There was virtually no preparation time allowed and so we really had no clue what would happen or how long it might run. I know this is considered heresy by today's serious standards, but it gave us hoots of laughter.

For example, I remember the cartoonist and crazy cockney Ben Wicks chose, from his list of three possibilities, the story of *My Fair Lady*. And he zoomed out of the gate, passionately galloping along with the details, actually getting one or two right, and then he just screeched to a halt. He explained how he had understood everything Eliza Doolittle said, right up to the point the professor got a hold of her.

One of the more crucial tasks of an interviewer is to silently, quickly and accurately assess the guest. Wicks and I have met fairly regularly over the years. Though I've left laughing every time, I knew from our first meeting that he was a man of substance and good will.

On the radio program *Fresh Air*, we taped "breakfasts" with guests. To make it sound like a kitchen and not the studio, we eagerly sought out and, truth be told, sometimes manufactured our own noise.

So here we are in Ben's beautiful condo in Toronto above the lake, and although he's well aware that the shtick is that he's supposed to serve me breakfast, I see he's gone to all the trouble of actually having made me a full cup of tea.

That's it. Not a lot of noise with a cup of tea. So the producer Gary Katz, wearing headphones and hearing only the subtlest sound of tea in a cup, keeps rattling the china and banging the spoon against the cup and saucer.

Wicks is too much of a pro not to speak into the microphone I'm holding out, but I see him more and more glancing with a kind of confused but concerned sideways look at Gary. I know he's thinking that the man has either lost his mind or is suffering from a disease as he continues to rattle everything on the coffee table before us.

The truth is Gary *is* laying it on a little thick and so I'm left to pray Wicks simply plays along until we're done, only a few minutes more.

Sometimes, there's nothing as pitiful as an unanswered prayer. Wicks has finally had enough and screams something along the lines of, "It sounds like the whole bloody condominium is in here having breakfast." The three of us, getting caught in the game of our own making, simply and completely collapsed in uncontrollable laughter.

Gary was left to do the necessary repairs on the tape as I was going to be away from the program that weekend. In fact, as we three giggling musketeers got into a cab to downtown Toronto, I was telling Ben that I would miss the broadcast of this epic breakfast because I was off to Bangladesh the next day, to a place called Cox's Bazaar.

I said I had never been and had no idea what to expect. Wicks looked concerned the way people do when you say you're traveling to a place named Cox's Bazaar in Bangladesh, and very kindly said something about being careful or taking it easy.

The timing of the cab driver was perfect. He turned around just as the silence in the back seat was long enough to be filled with private thoughts of danger and travel. With a big smile, he announced that Cox's Bazaar was his hometown and that it was really a beautiful holiday resort kind of place on the Bay of Bengal.

The last time I saw or heard Ben Wicks, he was screaming and shouting at me from the back of a cab in downtown Toronto about alleged hardship and foreign holiday spots. The driver just threw his head back and laughed. Wicks is a wonderful and generous man, except when it comes to breakfasts, and I always look forward to our next meeting.

One of the truly strange episodes of that summer in 1976 was a scheduled appearance by the folk singer Tim Hardin. We did the program live to the Maritimes between 3:00 and 5:00 in the afternoon Eastern time and it was then played across the country between 4:00 and 6:00. Whenever there was to be live music, which was almost every day, the rehearsal and sound checks were generally done between 2:00 and 3:00.

At about 2:30 on this one afternoon, Hardin still hadn't shown up and worry began to creep into the studio as he was supposed to be the guest for the whole first hour. Contingency plans were discussed and then dropped when, at about ten minutes to 3:00, Hardin showed up. Unfortunately, only in spirit – but what a spirit!

He was clearly so completely zonked out of his mind on something, we weren't too surprised when he announced he didn't know where he had left his guitar. Gary Katz, once again my trusted producer, quickly made the decision to forego the live music and instructed me just to sit down with Hardin, have a leisurely chat, and in between, whenever it was needed, we'd play some of his records. Sounded like a good plan to me. Confidence successfully transferred from G. Katz to P. Downie.

Hardin then saw an old album cover of his in my hands and the poor man started babbling incoherently about the picture on the front. The idea of a leisurely chat, arrived at just seconds before, was quickly losing its appeal, not to mention its possibility.

I must have looked terrified. Gary tried to reassure me by saying, "Look, it's Tim Hardin! Even if he throws up, it'll be interesting." Confidence shaky.

This is the classic difference between a host and a producer. I found astonishingly little of interest in the idea of Tim Hardin emptying his stomach on the radio and possibly on me. For his troubled sake, at least, Hardin was completely oblivious to the chaos he was causing all around him.

It was now minutes to the start of the show, with no guest for the first hour, and we could have simply put on a tape. But that would have been conceding defeat and so I raced to the CBC cafeteria to see if there was anybody hanging out there who could fill in for Hardin. I don't know how he felt about it, but this was my lucky day to stumble upon Manitoba folksinger Rick Neufeld.

I think he had just finished another show and was getting ready to leave when I collared him. The first hour of *The Entertainment Section* that day featured the live music of Rick Neufeld, who did an admirable job considering the conditions under which he was "invited" to appear.

The interview with Neufeld did, however, highlight another small problem. Katz refused to use a feature in the control room called "talk back," which allows the producer to do just that by holding down a switch and speaking directly into the host's head-sets. Gary preferred the "simpler" pen and card approach. He would hold up in the air a hastily scribbled note for me to try and read through the glass separating the control room from the studio.

Usually, Gary and I had no trouble with this kind of short-hand communication. But this hour he held up, more than once, a sign which simply read "Moody?" I thought to myself, "What a great producer to wonder kindly in the middle of the show if I'm still upset over the Hardin fiasco."

This illustrates yet another classic difference between a host and a producer. The host assumes his rightful position in the centre of the universe and simply understands that everything of consequence from the farthest flung corners of that universe has to do with him.

This time, though, Gary was asking, if it wasn't too much trouble, did I think I could ask Mr. Neufeld to play his hit *Moody Manitoba Morning*?

Not everyone was dragged to the studio to perform. It was not unusual to have visitors on tour come by to observe the program in progress. And so it wasn't a surprise one day to look up to see Gary virtually surrounded in the control room by a group of serious looking men in suits. I learned later that they were making such a noise that the usually shy Gary, trying to listen to the program, actually had to turn and ask them to lower their voices because he "couldn't hear" what was being said. Somebody in the tour group replied, raising his voice, " Oh sorry, I was just saying..."

The one day I remember Gary not being there was the day of, by far, my single worst interview in 25 years. To spare me torment, my brain has dutifully blocked out most of the details, but in broad strokes I can tell you it was a most unfortunate encounter with the writer John Fowles. Thank goodness, it was only on the phone and although scheduled for much longer, it ended within ten minutes.

I shoulder the blame for the disaster and, to this day, I feel the embarrassment and awkwardness of those awful moments on the phone. Fowles managed to push all the buttons that were already privately warning me that I was in over my head. I had survived up until then by that old "if I just keep dancing quickly enough, they won't notice" approach. Even Gary probably couldn't have saved me, but I surely missed his friendship that day. I will always remember Fowles as being, far and away, the single most ungracious, arrogant and rude radio guest I ever encountered.

The memory of that interview is eased a bit when I think of the people with whom I had good conversations on the radio that summer. Steve Martin was a new comic presence; Nora Ephron was a gifted, insightful and funny writer who shared her secrets on necking; Andrea Martin, Dave Thomas, Ben Gordon and Catherine O'Hara were just starting out; Milt Jackson was a jazz legend who performed live in the studio; actress Francis Hyland enchanted us with a story about her favorite tree; Martha Reeves performed after we frantically scrambled to rent drums for her band; and Sylvia Tyson with her band stole all the headphones one afternoon.

There was a virtual parade of mainly Canadian but also international performers and artists who graced that time period.

One who deserves more than passing mention was the delightfully generous Tom Wolfe, who filled me with confidence the way Fowles had drained it from me. I was beginning to learn how critical the first exchange with the guest is in a live situation. I always took tremendous care with that opening question knowing that a wrong one could set the entire conversation off kilter.

Walking down the corridor to the studio with Gary, fretting aloud about the Wolfe interview, his wise advice was this: "Why not ask Wolfe what section he would place his books in, in the library?"

It was close to a perfect opening and served as an invitation to Wolfe to be as playful as he wanted. He and I hit it off and I remember the hour just flying by. There's almost nothing in my life to compare with the rush that comes from such an experience. It is an exhilarating seduction, coaxing a little revelatory honesty from someone, and I was getting hooked on it.

There's something else worth mentioning here. These were hour-long conversations so they required homework and preparation. When they worked, it felt like sitting in front of a crackling fire with a careful lover and a bottle of Chateau Margeaux. When they *didn't* work, having your gums scraped was inviting by comparison.

You can't fake it for an hour, which might explain why this length of conversation has largely disappeared from the electronic media landscape. The phenomenon that is the writer and social observer Camille Paglia told me once that she was convinced the evolution of the human brain now allows it to handle much more information in split-second bursts than ever before. She thinks this is good. I'm not sure.

But if she's right, television has to answer for systematically reducing that attention span to the flicks of a remote control. There's no point getting all upset about this. The art of conversation simply doesn't matter to television, and probably never has.

I recall speaking to a group of seniors who were taking one of those "living and learning" courses at a university. I made my living in TV at the time and had been invited, as the host of CBC's *Man Alive*, to talk about why religious issues weren't dealt with by television. I did my best to explain what it was like to try to tackle important subjects in a medium that seemed to trivialize everything.

In the question and answer session which followed, a fellow at the back of the room stood to say that he had been among the first people involved with television when it began. He went on to explain that he didn't really understand all this hand-wringing because he and the other pioneers never expected it to be anything but entertainment. I sometimes think of his brevity in the face of the libraries now filled with learned essays and critiques of television's impact.

Allow me to jump ahead in the story for a moment to make a point about the importance of the length of these conversations. This, at first, might seem to contradict what was said in that classroom, but I think, in fact, it confirms it. When I hosted *Man Alive*, we prepared for the 25th Anniversary show by reviewing many of the previous episodes. Ironically it was that act which began my departure from the series.

What I saw so graphically over that 25-year period was a slow but steady turning away from presenting challenging thinkers and ideas, and an increasing reliance on cheap theatrics and shallow manipulations. *Man Alive* once stood out on television precisely because it alone offered the audience the equivalent of an elegant meal. By the time I got there, it was solidly headed for the fast food drive-thru window.

There is such a thing as the *art* of conversation and it is a skill I'm afraid we're losing in the marketplace of public dialogue. With hour-long interviews, we lived on that art at *The Entertainment Section*.

In an unusual move, Gzowski once invited me to watch as he prepared for a conversation with Gordon Lightfoot. In broad strokes, he mapped out the interview, showing me how to anticipate responses, how to plan directions, and generally how to get a feel and a sense of first, where you wanted it to go, and second, how to get there.

I came to think of it as a bit like building a house. Every builder needs the same basic material, supplied in radio's case by the producers and researchers. Then it's in the host's hands to put together a mansion, or something slightly more modest.

A few months of hour-long conversations certainly exercised my interview muscles and by the end of that summer in 1976 I was a different broadcaster than the guy who had arrived, just a few short months before, not-so-fresh from Fredericton.

The Entertainment Section challenged us intellectually and creatively and was a time in my life, and I think for my colleagues, which simply crackled with energy. Much of that energy came – again – from knowing who and what we were as public broadcasters. We took great pride in presenting programming unavailable elsewhere while understanding that would likely mean a smaller audience.

We were working in the same studio which was once home to Max Ferguson and Allan McFee and we couldn't resist the temptation to invite them back for an hour to reminisce about their time together. After all, legend was that it was in the suspended roof of this studio where Allan used to toss small bits of CBC equipment whenever the corporation "deserved it."

It was also where he apparently hooked up his car exhaust with a hose when somebody annoyed him.

If I was ever more nervous before an interview, I don't remember it.

I worried going into the hour that the major task facing me would be to simply try to exercise a tiny bit of control. Within seconds of the introductions, the hour was completely out of my hands.

Although I surely gave them ample opportunity to devour me, they both were tremendously kind and generous toward this young broadcaster with hair down to his waist. It was a lesson I never forgot.

I guess my nerves had shown during the hour with them and, when it was over and I started breathing again, Max took me aside to offer some advice regarding CBC management. " Don't let them break your spirit," was all he said. Little did I know then how central those six words would come to be in my career.

I have visited with Max a couple of times over the years and I've told him I didn't begin working in radio because of him, but he's the reason I lasted at the CBC as long as I did. His continued excellence on air in a place which, through bureaucratic sludge and myopic management, strives too often for mediocrity, is a grand testament to Max's spirit and immense talent.

By the end of that summer in 1976, it wasn't only my interviewing techniques which had grown. My ego had more than kept pace and I realized I had become exactly what I had asked Gzowski about a few years before in Fredericton.

I had wondered how he kept his ego in check because it would seem logical, I suggested to him, that sooner or later, the tables are reversed and it becomes the guest's job to find a way around the interviewer.

When *The Entertainment Section* was canceled, I had the time and some money to find my way around a bit of the world. For the first time and with wide eyes, I visited parts of England, Scotland, France, Spain, and Northern Africa.

I agree with Lance Morrow, who writes in his *Heart: A Memoir* that "We travel to lose ego, I suppose. To scrape the ego like the bottom of the boat and make the water run more sleekly past the hull. Or else to perform another sort of bypass on the heart, and make the blood flow more easily through it, the sympathies cleaner and clearer, the humility refurbished."

It's a bit embarrassing now to remember how I felt professionally on top of the world that September over 20 years ago, even as I had no job. Maybe I didn't stay away long enough or see the right things, but my first real travel didn't have quite the impact Morrow wrote about.

Returning to Canada on Halloween day in 1976, I clearly thought I was the cat's behind, confident of my abilities and ready to tackle whatever was to come my way next.

FIVE

THE WEST

"Next" turned out to be a kind of hands-on education about the role of the CBC and its potential impact across the country. This is probably obvious, but perhaps it needs to be said clearly: I believe the essence of the CBC should be to reflect, explain, and celebrate one part of this vast land to another. It should be a place by and for Canadians and in every way, at every turn, it must struggle to present the complexities of the Canadian sensibility and reality.

This too needs to be said unequivocally: television, long ago, abandoned even the pretense of performing this role. It now seems to be the permanent home of juvenile comedians, both intentional and unintentional. I know how difficult it is to host a program and it is not my desire to level direct criticism at any one person. But in a general way, I think there are people now in hosting positions on CBC television who would not even have made a long "short list" ten years ago. Television attracts show-offs and as it increasingly dominates our culture, these show-offs suddenly start to believe they're also important. What a deadly mixture.

So we now have the self-important "investigative" types out to set the world straight or, more recently, CBC producers who have started to hire professional actors to front programs. How much clearer could it be that while television is seen, more and more, as the great validator of life, it is seen by those who make it as theater?

There was a time when you could skip through the television channels and know almost immediately when you had landed on the CBC because it was immediately apparent that the content was unique to the public broadcaster. The slow but sure embrace by Canadians of American-style market force determinism has almost destroyed public television to the extent now that it's virtually indecipherable from all the other mindless pablum served up as television entertainment.

Please don't get me wrong. Some of my favorite programs are made of pablum, but when it comes to *public* broadcasting, I dedicated my working life, until recently, to trying to make sure it held itself to a different standard. We've reached the point in Canada where a program which is doing exactly what it should be doing – *Adrienne Clarkson Presents* – is often criticized as an example of how lost the CBC has become. I think Adrienne's program does what it does well and should survive, despite smallish audiences, precisely because no one else will present the material which she does.

To my mind, CBC television has utterly failed in its primary task, which is to reflect and celebrate who we are *as Canadians* – not as wannabe Americans. Working in television can be intoxicating for those seeking power. The opportunity and temptation to compare ourselves with the omnipresent American television juggernaut is rarely passed up and I'm afraid the corporation, wanting to be thought of as playing in the "big leagues," has begun to copy American program models and sensibilities.

Would anyone with a sense of who *we* are as Canadians cancel programs like *Tommy Hunter* or *Rita MacNeil?* Decisions like these are not surprising when the network is run by people who believe the only important things in this country happen within the borders of Metropolitan Toronto. This is not a defense of Tommy or Rita. They don't need that. It is a plea for CBC television to stop aping American-style programs.

We have all the confidence and talent necessary in this country to fill every hour with unique, interesting and vital *Canadian* programming. Ours is a vast land which, in many ways, is still waiting to be explored and reflected on television. Our national character is different from that of our American neighbors. Surely with the proper will, CBC television can do a much better job of helping all Canadians to understand the unlimited wealth, richness and potential of this country. But you can't do that from behind a desk in good old Toronto.

Like a lemming approaching that cliff by the ocean, I'm afraid radio is close enough now to see the splash from television's belly flop. If the fundamental direction of radio isn't changed, and soon, I fear that it too runs the risk of becoming irrelevant.

It's almost reached the point now that if you want a second cup of coffee in St. John's, you have to get the okay from some soulless bureaucrat in Toronto. Let me give you one small example of where it's gone wrong. In the fall of 1996, a series of interviews had been arranged for me with the hosts of various CBC radio morning shows across the country. I was promoting my book *Healers at Work* and looked forward to the CBC interviews because, well, because it still feels like home to me.

I wasn't surprised that, without exception, the CBC hosts I met over the phone were good, smart, quality broadcasters and I confess that the whole experience was like finding a friend in a crowd of strangers. But the friend had changed and was no longer as familiar as before.

With the exception of one or two brave souls, these morning show hosts all read the same introduction and asked the same questions in the same order. They were following a line of questioning and thinking faxed overnight from Toronto.

Answering the same questions over and over obviously made it easier for me. It was surely easier for the local hosts not to have to read the book or think of questions themselves, and clearly it is more efficient, in terms of control, when all "wisdom" flows from Toronto. Who needs the researchers and producers in the troublesome regions if some master plan can be devised, e-mailed and followed across the country?

My sense is that with the budget cuts, almost everyone is afraid of losing their job. And so the regional backlash that this kind of central control deserves – and would have received even 10 years ago – simply hasn't happened.

This is not to say that the network doesn't have an important role to play, but it seems to me to be like a fresh-water lake where the rivers flowing in are suddenly choked off. It doesn't take very long for that lake to become stagnant. If the current strangulation of the regional "rivers" of the CBC continues, the centre will become lifeless.

I do believe, as I say, that that centre still has a role to play. There used to be something almost magical for me driving across the prairies under the weight of that enormous sky or meandering through a little town in Prince Edward Island, colored by a rainbow of greens in mid-summer, and hearing the distinctive voice of Rex Loring reading the news. The power of that shared experience of listening, regardless of where you are in the land, should never be underestimated or ignored. But it is the regions which form the skeleton of the CBC.

You could always count on the CBC's local shows to consistently provide quality information. More often than not, they also provided a thoughtful and articulate reflection of the community in which these shows lived and operated – both within that community and, on the larger network, to the rest of the country when requested. I think the kind of creeping homogenization of the CBC underway now has put this role in peril.

This loss of diversity at the C.B.C is a profound one and I think it has parallels in the natural world. John Livingston, who began, incidentally, *The Nature of Things* on CBC television, has written in his book *Rogue Primate* that, "There is a growing creeping and crawling sameness that is the utter antithesis of ecological and evolutionary process. Sameness and simplicity are the two hallmarks of domestication."

There are a number of reasons why the CBC is abandoning its regional role and budget cuts are a factor. But let's be clear about this: it's the CBC which has chosen *where* to make the cuts and it alone is responsible for the slow strangulation now underway.

When I moved to Calgary in 1976, I didn't know very much about the west. Like so many others from the east, I had hitchhiked there in summer to find work in places like Banff and Lake Louise and Trail, B.C., so the picture I had of life there was more of a postcard than a portrait. As an employee of the CBC, I was lucky enough to learn about very different parts of the country but I worry sometimes if listeners ever get the same benefit.

The actor Barry Morse said to me one afternoon in Calgary that as soon as he left the plane he was struck by the size of the sky. It filled him with a kind of exuberance that anything was possible in this western "get up and go atmosphere." I realized at that moment that I was, at heart, an easterner and possibly, with even more luck, an honorary maritimer.

The weight of potential is not something I carry enthusiastically or voluntarily. It seems wiser to me to expect the worst and be surprised by anything pleasant which occurs by accident. As you can imagine, this makes me a really big hit at parties. Come to think of it, it's probably why the last party I went to was in 1969. Once, in the middle of negotiations with a CBC television manager, when (by most accounts) my career was sailing along, I was grumbling about this and that and he accused me of being a Cape Bretoner! It is still the nicest thing any CBC boss ever said to me.

I didn't have much luck hiding my eastern roots from Albertans. There were the obvious clues, such as my inability to understand the entertainment value of watching a man sit on a bull for as long as he could, or jump off a horse and wrestle to tie the legs of a calf. I appreciate there's a rich history to this and I don't dismiss that heritage. It just didn't mean much to me.

I started going out with a lovely woman whose parents owned a houseboat on Shuswap Lake, in B.C., and a place outside Calgary I learned to call a ranch and not a cottage – the unfortunate extent of my "western-ness" then and now. Her father got a great laugh when he sent me out for the first time with a bucket of oats to feed their three horses at the ranch.

The three "Mr. Eds" were standing on the other side of this huge field ... ah, pasture. They zeroed in on me – actually the pail – and started to run toward the goodies. I've always thought it smart not to tell something that big what to do and, as the size of the three of them grew bigger and they got closer and closer until I could see something or other coming out their noses, I just knew they were going to rip out my jugular vein, then bite and kick me to death.

When they put the brakes on and started to nudge me aside to get their snoots in the pail, I had had enough. I dropped the pail and, it being far too late for any degree of nonchalance, ran inside. Her father shook his head with a kind of bemused sadness.

We would often drive to the houseboat, my girlfriend and I, for a few days to enjoy the great beauty of Shuswap Lake. The first time we went we couldn't get the motor to start even though I kept checking the fuel tank. It was on the right side of the boat and it was easy, even for an easterner, to verify its level by lowering a measuring stick into the pontoon and seeing clearly the wet mark left by the fuel.

We had plenty, almost a full tank I realized, and yet the motor turned and turned and turned without starting.

Even though I began with a fierce determination not to bother or announce to her already skeptical father back in Calgary that I couldn't even get the motor going, I started to weaken as the afternoon sun faded and we faced the prospect of spending our first night on the boat tied to the dock.

Judging that the humiliation was potentially more acute from having the marina owner watching us settle in for the night attached to land, she called her father. "Who knows," I reassured myself, "maybe there *is* really something wrong with the engine and I might regain some lost credibility by telling him about it so quickly."

My friend returned from the phone, stifling a giggle. The waste tank was located on the *right* side of the boat. A quick calculation, then, would put the fuel tank on the left side. I, of course, had spent the better part of the afternoon verifying the level of waste and wasn't entirely surprised when the left tank came up bone dry. We put some fuel in the tank on the left and just like that, we were on our way, chugging off into a lovely western sunset, as far away as possible from the echo of laughter from Calgary.

I became restless and uneasy in Alberta and wanted desperately to head back east. For better or for worse, I came to understand, my heart and soul belonged in Quebec. After quitting my job in Calgary, I found myself for the first, but not the last, time in my life out of work. I didn't have a clue how to use that time in a way that was even remotely helpful or valuable in coming to do the inner work I needed to tackle. And so I spent it in much the same way as my entire time in Alberta – partying and having a good time.

And it *was* a good time. You're going to have to look elsewhere for a story of regret and redemption. I managed to waste time and money magnificently. I was irresponsible, selfish and self-indulgent. My only true regret is that I wasn't wise enough to know the value of the love I felt for the woman who shared my life, and I didn't feel settled enough to accept hers. That, and the fact I still owe Norm Hurley of CBC Calgary money for season's tickets to the Stampeders.

Two things strike me most powerfully from a professional point of view following my experience in Calgary. First, the CBC then offered many options to young broadcasters, even to those who, like me, would occasionally quit. There was a constant flow of new blood coming through the doors. It was alive and vibrant and creative.

Second, the national vision of the corporation included strong, independent and vigorous regional expressions. And as discussed before, we all lose when denied access to those expressions and realities.

Between CBC radio and television, the former has always been praised and held above the latter, occasionally for good reason. But if radio wants to expand beyond its fairly constant core audience, it had better reverse the trend and start to listen and manage from the regions inward.

The best lesson I ever had in this was in Sudbury, Ontario, where CBC radio was setting up an operation headed by my old friend from the University of New Brunswick, Bill Akerley.

Despite my previously undistinguished attempt at producing, I went to work for Bill as the producer of the brand new morning show in Sudbury called *Morning North*. It was there that I did one of the best things I've ever done for the CBC and that was to hire Benita Hart.

I'm not someone who makes friends easily, but quite quickly Bea and I became and remain very close, even though there has been much time and distance between us. She's smart and a very hard worker, but I think what I respect most about her is her sense of ethical living. She knows who she is, what she cares about, what matters and, just as importantly, what doesn't. I've learned a great deal from her over the years about justice and fairness and the rarity of true and simple friendship.

We had quite a little morning program underway in Sudbury and on a number of occasions I'd recall something the program director in Calgary said to me: "You know, Peter, the problem with you is you think you have to like the people you work with."

I think that was a fair assessment. Given the climate at CBC Calgary then and the fact that it was identified as a problem goes some way in explaining why I wanted to get out of there. CBC Sudbury wasn't old enough to have festering personal feuds and divided loyalties, so friendships were formed quickly and it was invigorating to have everyone pulling in the same direction.

In some ways, Sudbury was a return to my beginnings in New Brunswick. The people at the station and in the community of Sudbury were very much like those in Fredericton. I settled into a lovely place on Ramsey Lake Road where, in the evenings, I could lie in bed and listen to the loons chatter on the lake.

I knew I was going to enjoy my time in Sudbury by the way I got a fridge for my new place. The senior technician at the station had a cottage on one of the incredible number of lakes surrounding the city and he had a friend of a friend of a friend who had a fridge for sale. The only catch was we had to go and get it by boat.

It started out well – a little chilly heading out across the water, but all in all, a good bargain with the fridge and a great way to see a bit of the geography of my new home. The long backbone of the Canadian shield would occasionally rise along the shores of these lakes and I always saw them as resting whales whose backs broke the water to enjoy the warmth of the sun.

No sun on fridge-day, unfortunately. We picked it up, balanced it precariously in the fairly small boat and, as the wind picked up and the temperature dropped, Eckhart and I started back across the lake.

We got all of ten feet from shore before the storm struck. The sleet hit our face and hands like a million razor blades hurling through space and our knuckles took on a lovely rose hue, a mixture of white, from holding onto the fridge and our lives, and red, from the frigid splashing water whipped up by a frozen wall of wind. My kind of town.

At a fairly rowdy dinner one night not so long ago, held, incidentally, to celebrate the opening of a photographic exhibit by my former radio producer Anne Bayin, we were comparing places where we had lived. I said I knew it sounded trite, but that I'd never forget the warmth and generosity and welcoming spirit of the people in Sudbury. The fellow across from me just about jumped over the table with excitement to say that's how Regina is for him.

I wondered, later that night, about how lucky any one of us is to enjoy that great happiness and security which comes from feeling like we belong to a community, to have the chance to experience that kind of uncomplicated love and warmth and acceptance at least once in our lives. I fell asleep with the conclusion that, in the end, it is not everything we are about. It is the *only* thing.

I would guess that half my salary in Sudbury went for veterinarian bills as my beloved cat, Moe, got into a fight every other day under the porch with the neighbor's cat, Nutsy – for good reason. One night at dusk, the two of them were at it again and, in my dressing gown, I ran outside with the broom to break them up. Having separated them, I started climbing back over the rocks that covered the floor of the forest in front of the house when Nutsy actually charged me. I figured it wouldn't be long before Moe and I would get run out of town by that lunatic feline. And Moe almost hadn't made it in the first place.

When I left Calgary for Sudbury, my girlfriend kept the two cats, Moe and Eddie, with her, until I found a place and settled in a new home. The plan was that she would then fly with the two cats to Sudbury. She got a flight for the three of them, with a stopover in Thunder Bay. We spoke when she was there and everything seemed to be fine.

About an hour later, she landed in Sudbury and we waited for the cats to be unloaded. And we waited. And we waited. And then the plane took off. No cats. I was beside myself with worry and couldn't believe Moe and Ed, two live cats, had just vanished.

By the next afternoon, Air Canada had traced them to Toronto. It turns out that of the two destination stickers on top of the cages, the handler in Sudbury had chosen to read the old one from when they had flown to Toronto from New Brunswick. So the cats paid for my mistake by spending a night in the big city before coming home. And when they did reach Sudbury, they both took about three steps from the cage and then fell over and slept for the next 12 hours. As did I.

I'm not sure how good I was at producing this time around, but we sure seemed to have a lot of fun putting *Morning North* together every day. My old boss in Calgary had been absolutely correct. It was important to me that people got along and that approach seemed sensible and worthwhile if better work was the goal.

I don't know about other professionals, but journalists can spend hours and hours talking about the work. I suppose I took part in those kinds of discussions early on but not so much by the time I was producing in Sudbury. Part of the attraction for me was that at one second past nine, when the program was done for that morning, it was done. I'd expect that we'd all work like crazy to find and to form the words and to put a show together, but once it was sent off into space, we'd get to start with a fresh slate the next day.

I liked the job of producing this time around and even managed to learn some of its benefits, but, in my heart, I knew it wasn't what I could do for very long. I used to joke that I was getting bumps on my head from lunging at the window separating the studio from the control room. As a host, I had always expected to receive respect from the producer. As a producer, I now had to learn to give the same respect to someone else.

The anniversary of Elvis Presley's death afforded me an opportunity to learn that lesson. I asked Benita if she'd like to do a little essay on Elvis at the end of the next program.

As I now recall it, she eagerly accepted my invitation and I looked forward to hearing her thoughts. What I *didn't* do was produce her script in the morning, trusting that she would have pleasant, innocuous stories of growing up listening to Elvis.

When it came time for this two-minute remembrance, B.'s first sentence was something like, "Elvis Presley was a bloated, drugged, and pathetic victim of rapacious American capitalism..." In a split second I knew we weren't likely to be hearing stories about swivelling hips on Ed Sullivan. But it brought sharply into focus the truth that, as a producer of this kind of feature, it wasn't *my* opinion which counted. This knowledge would set me on a collision course for later work in television when producers would treat hosts as microphone stands with lips, but all it did in Sudbury on that morning was cause another collision with the studio glass.

When Bill Akerley left Sudbury as manager, I was the only one around who had been with the CBC longer than five minutes, so I became the *acting* manager. What a role it turned out to be, one for which I never did quite learn the proper lines. I remember almost nodding off in budget talks with suits from Toronto who spoke of the station as a physical plant. There were also arguments about who got which desk in the French newsroom, and once, when my boss from Toronto paid a visit, he ended the day by going to see *Apocalypse Now* for some relief from his day with us at CBC Sudbury. Oh, the horror.

While producing felt like one step removed from the action, acting as a manager meant I needed binoculars just to see the producers. I spent almost all my time on stuff not even remotely connected to broadcasting, so I got a bit fidgety with no creative outlet. Instead, I decided to continue the guitar lessons I had abandoned in Montreal at the age of nine and also to return to my love of painting by taking drawing lessons from the husband of the manager of the French side of things at CBC Sudbury.

He and I had never met when he asked me over the phone to submit a drawing of some kind for an article in the local paper about his upcoming course. The drawing, he explained, would illustrate better than words any progress I might make as a student of his.

I had been listening to a historical album narrated by Edward R. Murrow and, at home that night, I drew a sketch of Murrow from the cover of the album and sent it off to the teacher the next morning. That week in the *Sudbury Star*, there was this sketch of an elderly man with the caption "Peter Downie – Self-Portrait" underneath. While I was ensuring my anonymity, I grew to love and feel at home in Northern Ontario.

It's an odd conclusion for someone born in the suburbs of Montreal, but Sudbury – with all the lakes and forests and wildlife around the city – kind of confirmed for me that my comfort level has become directly proportional to the degree of wilderness around me.

I'm not sure where or how that began, except one of my earliest memories is of fishing with my father in the Eastern Townships of Quebec. He would tell me stories about the woods and the animals as we slowly drifted along this secluded creek. I imagine my eyes grew as big as his whispered "lies" about the bears and cougars watching us float by.

One of the first places I visited in Quebec, after my recent departure from the CBC and my starting down this new path, was that river where my father and I had "escaped" almost 35 years ago. The tears that came to my eyes made me feel like a little boy with grass-stained knees again.

On this visit, it was my spirit which felt stained by experience. Being at that spot, this many years later, also confirmed something terribly important to me. My life *was*, indeed, starting over again. And if I could only learn to control the terror of it all and to avoid the temptation to simply jump back on the job merry-go-round, in time the lines of the circle would meet and I could begin to feel whole once more.

Even though those early fishing trips with my father weren't repeated in later years, as I got older, I began to realize I was consistently less disappointed by the natural world than by human beings, to the extent now that I take it as a compliment when accused of being a hermit. I can't imagine a spring without being close enough to nature to hear the joyous, returning song of the red-winged blackbirds or to feel the sponginess of the thawing earth squishing underfoot.

The forest by my old house in Sudbury became a virtual cathedral in the fall, with its very particular and beautiful kind of silence as winter approached. Tall pines and trembling aspen would meet at the sky and I'd often stand there alone, under this canopy, in wonder and awe at the power of creation. My dog would then drop a ball at my feet and we'd carry on to-gether toward the river where we could play on the ice. I'd be Rocket Richard and she'd be defenceman "Dog" Harvey.

So aside from the wonderful people I met and the lasting friendships made, and despite the daily presence of Nutsy the cat, Sudbury also offered this kind of inspiring geography which nourished me and naturally felt like home. There are only two other places whose landscape has had a similar impact on me.

One is a spot on Prince Edward Island where no one else ever seems to go but it is a memory and image I invoke on the darkest and coldest winter nights. The ocean, the sand, those beautiful rounded dunes holding onto the most stubborn look-ing pines in the world, with the prickly grass at their feet wav-ing in the warm summer wind, a sky the color of faded jeans, the gentle clouds, the broken shells, the dried-out seaweed, the shrieking plovers, and, of course, the row of gulls looking like Supreme Court Justices in a line-up against the ever-present wind. It is a place that refreshes all senses.

The other spot is near Fort Fitzgerald on the border of the Territories and Alberta. Other observers far more eloquent than I have written of this attachment *to* and sense *of* the land, but I never truly felt it until standing along the Great Slave River one after-noon. I have never thought about Canada in the same way again. We are, I believe, informed as a people by our wilderness and shaped by the ruggedness of our land, whether we're drifting on Hearn Lake in the Territories with loons by the side of the boat, or searching for our car at a huge shopping mall in Mississauga.

One chilly night in Kiev, Ukraine, I stood in a town square shivering as a demonstration was held for survivors of the

Chernoble nuclear tragedy. A young Ukrainian boy came over and in almost perfect English started a conversation by asking if I wanted to borrow a sweater. When he learned I was Canadian, he looked surprised and said, "But you're from the north like me, you should be able to handle this cold."

A more industrial landmark on the geography facing me everyday in Sudbury was that blessed Inco smokestack but my time in its shadow taught me about the value of compromise and the price paid by single industry towns.

That sometimes uneasy relationship between business and workers is not presented often in its full spectrum by a media which is hungry for simplistic black and white, stereotypical situations and characters. This "good guys/bad guys" approach precludes much thoughtful and fair reporting on the strange tango that takes place between the business and the community when there's only one major employer in the area, like Inco.

There was still a sliver of hope for CBC television in those days, because it at least placed some value on telling Canadian stories. I remember a movie starring Al Waxman, about the cost of unemployment in a one-industry community like Sudbury. They obviously wanted some publicity and offered Waxman as a guest to appear on our CBC morning radio show. I said, "Sure, if we screen the show with members of the local steel-workers' union," who were already on strike against Inco.

To Waxman's credit, he showed up, watched the movie with the workers, and spent a couple of hours afterward speaking with them and us. I thought, and still do, that he showed a lot of class that day when it would have been far easier for him to have stayed in the safety of Toronto and done an interview over the phone.

Just as my experiences in Woodstock, New Brunswick, had taught me to respect the power of the microphone and not to say anything to it which I wouldn't say to someone in person, Waxman confirmed and cemented that idea of accountability forever to my professional life.

Speaking of which, I would never have left Sudbury save for my ambition. I don't for a second believe it could have been different, but I have wondered since if placing my job and ego and all that ahead of more personal happiness was worth it.

But the sad truth was – the past tense is hopeful – that my work was what made me happy. I never really expected that central part of me to be satisfied by anything or anyone else. So was it because only the work could push those buttons, or because I only let work near them?

I don't know the complete answer to that. The partial answer is that I was *not* a miserable, kidnapped worker. I got great satisfaction and derived much happiness from my profession during this time. I suppose, had I been able to keep it going, I may never have realized just how much of a central role it was playing in my life and in defining who I was – to myself and to others. I regard it as a sign of health that I couldn't keep going the way I always had been.

Maybe all of us who hear a calling go through those years when the work has to be paramount. All I've come to understand, for myself, is that there is a price to be paid for that pursuit and, when it's all said and done, I'm hoping the rewards of a cared for and nourished inner life can be far more valuable and lasting. But in the middle of a hurricane, it's hard to acknowledge the stillness.

So there I sat, first as a producer, getting lumps on my head, and then with the headaches that came from sitting at the manager's desk, feeling a million miles away from the business I thought myself in. The choice was clear to me. If I wanted to save my head, I had to get behind a microphone again.

Around this time, in Montreal, Katie Malloch decided to leave the afternoon show called *Home Run*. I wasn't crazy about doing yet another 4:00-6:00 p.m. show, but the really attractive idea, aside from hosting again, was being back home for the approaching referendum called by Rene Levesque and his Parti Quebecois. I applied and moved.

I had not really been in Montreal since leaving for the University of New Brunswick in 1968. It's hardly a bulletin that it wasn't the same place when I returned in 1980. Not surprisingly, the tension of the referendum campaign was literally everywhere. It couldn't be escaped.

Years later, I would ask Levesque if he thought he had been judged more harshly for having lost a dream as opposed to just another political project. He stunned me when he replied that it was never a dream for him. He explained he had always and only seen it as a "plan." Well, that was not the truth on the ground. This was clearly the dream of a generation and the eventual loss of the *Oui* side devastated some of my new colleagues and strained any relationship between us for some time.

Away from politics, Montreal was still Montreal – meaning that life and not work was the priority to be pursued vigorously and passionately. I met the writer H. Gordon Greene during this time, when I rented a house from him on his farm in Ormstown. When I said I'd take the four-bedroom place, he said he only wanted "the chance to share the women with me." I didn't know Gordon yet and so was a bit taken aback by his comment, but I soon came to learn it was a playful part of his role as a kind of professional "dirty old man."

I learned a lot about living in the country and energy for life from Gordon, but apparently not enough about the workings of a water pump. The belt had broken and the motor ran until it burned itself out, which would only have been an expensive annoyance in July. But this was a bone-chilling February and when the pump stopped, the pipes froze. Solid. After about a month of no water and imposing on friends for the basics, the freezing weather still hadn't let up. As a last resort, Gordon and his helper and I went to the basement to try to get some heat into the pipes. The plan, for some reason, was to undo a section of the exit waste pipe.

As the helper struggled with the wrench on the pipe, Gordon and I stood off to the side. By a mere fluke, I happened to be further away from the pipe in question than was the instruction-yelling Mr. Greene. When the thing virtually exploded apart with all the pressure of a month of ... ah, waste, Gordon took a full frontal bath. He was last seen climbing the basement stairs, barking, "You're a salty bastard, Downie."

Gordon raised what are called Belted Galloway cattle and their markings are quite striking – a black body with a wide white stripe or belt around their middle. They also seemed much friskier than other cattle I had observed up close and so we had a constant daily battle in the summer to keep them from licking and chewing on the barbecue on my back porch.

There was also a lovely crab apple tree just across the stone fence on my property which they would regularly kick and stumble over to get to the treats which had fallen to the ground. This act was always followed by the appearance of a screaming and swearing Gordon, waving his hands in the air to get the cows back home.

I was breezing along at work, making new and good friends and generally pleased to be back home in Montreal and Quebec. I moved a couple of times and was now in an old brick house far from the road. My father came from Toronto for an unusual visit one summer day and we sat on the porch, sipping cool drinks, looking over the farmer's fields, listening to the sounds of a sizzling summer afternoon in the country.

I had not been particularly close to my father, but that seemed to be changing and this visit went some way toward us getting to know each other a bit. He had stopped in on his way to Kennebunkport, Maine, for a short vacation. When he left, I looked forward to a planned golf game we had arranged to play in Toronto in a couple of weeks.

That night, I stood on the porch thinking how remarkable it was that he had actually visited when a feeling came over me that, to this day, is hard to describe. I remember clearly staring up at these enormous thunder clouds rumbling overhead as the rays of the late afternoon sun cut through the sky like shards of crystal glass falling from heaven's dinner table. The feeling which overcame me wasn't frightening or welcoming. It was simply very, very powerful.

Within the week, my father was dead. I don't know that there's any connection between losing him and what happened on that porch, in that sky, on that summer evening, but here it is, more than 17 years later, and the hairs on the back of my neck stand up as the memory returns.

I was aware that his death had an impact on my work and I learned that, for all these years, I had really just wanted to make him proud of me. I've been heartened since by meeting other men who shared that desire to be loved and recognized by a father. The poet Patrick Lane has written of setting a field on fire, knowing that his father would punish him with a beating, but accepting it as, at least, a kind of attention from him.

Now that my own father was gone so suddenly, it was the first time in my adult life that I felt a deep and profound regret over what might have been.

Soon after his death, I left the local afternoon show in Montreal to host *Cross Country Check-Up* on the CBC radio network, easily one of the toughest jobs I've ever had. What I learned very quickly is that the vast majority of people don't phone a radio program to share and explore ideas. They either call to inflict their "truth" on everyone else or they have an axe to grind. More likely, a combination of both. Either way, I would go from Sunday to Sunday never really sure of how things would turn out. That uncertainty led to superstitions.

For example, good weather on Sundays would always scare me because, I figured, who is it that prefers phoning a radio program to being in the sunshine? This was well before talk radio had become the rage and *Cross Country* was the only national phone-in show in Canada. I have all kinds of admiration for radio talk show hosts but not for the increasing number who deliberately try to anger and provoke people. It is the ultimate victory of sizzle and only the station owner profits. It's exploitative, incendiary, and while pretending to honor the so-called "common" person's opinion, it instead treats everyone like a moron. If I hear one more ten-cent psychologist peddling greeting card platitudes while using clearly troubled individuals as entertainment, I might even change the channel.

Why is it that people will call and unload the worst personal stories of infidelity and betrayal and despair in public? And why am I listening to it? There are all the quick and easy answers about the breakdown of the family and the community unit which once provided support for these people. I've listened to the arguments that the church in many cases is virtually without influence and, in the end, it's unfortunate that people love to hear about others who are worse off than themselves.

Fine. There's probably a grain of truth in all of those stock answers, but I don't think it gets anywhere close to explaining why our media – mostly television, but also talk radio and many magazines and newspapers – has become utterly obsessed with society's bottom feeders.

Is it possible that our lives in North America have become so boring, empty, meaningless, and without direction that we devour sensationalism like demented kids locked over a long weekend in the candy store? It appears to be so. Except those who don't worry about life in this way would never consider themselves empty or without direction, so the cycle just continues. If an unexamined life falls in the forest, who cares if anyone takes notice?

The great god of television now rules and is the arbiter of importance in our culture. The supreme compliment today is to be told your performance was "Oprah-like." A talk show host – a talk show host! – has become the benchmark of excellence. We need look no further to explain the corrosion of values in our society.

As I write these words, the Red River in Manitoba is threatening all in its path and the television images are as compelling as they are heartbreaking. Neighbors are virtually arm in arm trying to protect themselves and their property. *This* is when television works. *This* is when words can't begin to match the force of image. I only wish the various anchors and reporters didn't seem quite so excited by it. When used poorly, as it almost always is in situations like this, television trivializes everything. The result is staged interviews with red-eyed people literally shaking from exhaustion and emotion, being asked "How does it feel to lose everything?"

It's partly television's technical demands which require the asking of such simple questions, but it's little wonder cynicism in and toward the media is as high as the Red River. I actually just heard the *perfect* television question a couple of nights ago. CBS's Dan Rather was interviewing the lawyer who had represented the just-condemned-to-death terrorist, Timothy McVeigh. Rather was quoting from one of McVeigh's letters which said to government officials, in part, "Die, you cowardice [sic] bastards!" Rather looked up and, with a straight face, asked, "What did McVeigh mean by that?"

I remember reading once the observation that the real danger with rampant cynicism, when people lose confidence in each other and with their institutions, is not that we believe in nothing. Precisely the opposite. It is then that we will believe *anything*.

As I listen to private talk radio these days I keep thinking about how what entertains us changes. I can't help thinking that we've been totally consumed – largely through television – by consumerism and, as a result, we have become restlessly and aggressively impatient about almost everything.

We ignore the value of the *journey* to concentrate only on the cost of the destination. We think we can buy happiness and meaning like we choose a chocolate bar, or that we can pick up some inner calm and peace like we whip through the drive-thru lane at a fast food restaurant. Human McBeings. After all, time is all we've got, but the modern disease, as the late Sir Laurens Van der Post described it to me once, is that we see it as something to be overcome.

When I listen to talk radio today, and I do, I search the stations I get in this area for even a smidgen of personal and/or social responsibility mentioned. I look for a trace of morality or ethical judgment included in any of the daily posturing and screaming. I'm not talking about preaching here. I only want a serious discussion of an important topic related to leading a life of worth. I come up empty, and, while I don't know, I suspect that that's true elsewhere.

If you take away the anger, the sarcasm, the bitterness, and the blind, paranoid fury whipped up by the verbal bully behind the microphone, you have nothing left but an electronic hum, a kind of sad, modern heartbeat.

For my money, and yours come to think of it, it is only *Cross Country Check-Up* which consistently delivers smart people exchanging and debating legitimate, well thought out points of view at the national level. I don't think there's another program in the country which can give you such an immediate and accurate sense of our incredible diversity.

One of the earliest topics we tackled, during my time as host, was the tragic civil war then raging in Lebanon. The complexity of that situation, with all the various warring factions, was mind-boggling and I worried, as we began that Sunday afternoon, if we weren't going to end up burying ourselves, getting bogged down with the tiniest, most obscure details of an ageless, passionate conflict on the other side of the world.

It wasn't the first or last time I would be amazed by the awareness and the passion of Canadians. That afternoon, I remember well, featured a hot debate between a Sunni and a Shiite Muslim – one at each end of Canada. As it was going on, I was too busy being a referee to really enjoy the action, but on my way home that night I smiled thinking of how much richer and more interesting our national community actually is than the portrait presented by the smug, almost completely white upper-class media elite of Toronto.

One light but troubling moment in preparing for the show which I would remember later came from the New York Times' Thomas Friedman in his excellent book, *From Beirut to Jerusalem*. If you haven't read it yet I highly recommend it to you. He tells of being taken into one of the mountain ranges outside Beirut and being stopped by one militia group and having an AK 47 stuck in his ribs by a fierce-looking character.

Friedman writes, with great eloquence, that he was certain his life was about to end after revealing he was an American citizen. His would-be killer broke into a wide grin and asked, "So who shot J.R.?"

I don't remember *Cross Country Check-Up* having many deliberately funny moments and more often than not, I shared with Friedman that fear of imminent demise. The two-hour show was a bit like the proverbial snowball at the top of the hill which, once gently nudged, picks up speed, becomes larger and larger, and, before you know it, is unstoppable.

In a kind of reverse of the task facing Sisyphus, the host of *Cross Country* can either jump out of the way or attempt to direct this giant mass to a safe landing at the bottom of the hill. "Jumping out of the way" was, I suspect, a universal fantasy shared by *Cross Country* hosts. It was one of mine which was left, alas, unfulfilled. I got advice from former hosts. One took me aside to say, "Whatever you do, avoid Jews in space!"

"Excuse me?"

"Avoid any war or conflict involving Israel," he explained, "and the Middle East."

Another former host told me of how a guest once "jumped out of the way" of the show. Actually, I gather, it was more like racing to the bathroom during a long diatribe from an angry caller. The guest rushed back to his seat just in time to hear the caller yell, "So what do you think of that?"

"There's much in what you say," was his answer. Or so the story goes.

Cross Country Check-Up has been on the air for over 30 years. It got its name, incidentally, because the first show was on Canada's health care system and the "check-up" part just stuck. What makes the direction of it trickier than most programs is the lack of relief.

There's no music which can give you a couple of minutes to collect your thoughts and there's no newscast to give you a break. I guess it was surviving its relentless nature which made it great fun when it worked. But when it didn't go well and skidded off the tracks we had so carefully laid, I would get home feeling like a punching bag.

Part of the problem was it happened only once a week, so it was difficult to build an ongoing relationship with an audience, which, for me, is the essence of broadcasting.

I missed the demands and the interplay of a daily program where, if one part of it fails, you have a chance to move on to something else quite quickly. Once I announced the question on *Cross Country*, there was no turning back. I couldn't change it half way through even if it was desperately and obviously wrong, although I confess that rarely happened.

I worked with a producer on the program once who was, half jokingly, constantly suggesting "Do you like tomato sandwiches?" as a kind of generic *Cross Country* question. His idea was we could start there and see what developed. There were Sundays when I heartily agreed with him.

There are two *Cross Country Check-up* programs which stand out in my mind. The first was broadcast live from Prince Albert in Northern Saskatchewan. The premiers of the provinces had been meeting at a nearby resort and we had decided on the question, "Should the provinces have more power?"

Our guest was to be the host premier, Allan Blakeney. But we all awoke in the hotel that Sunday morning without any power – electrical that is. So after trips up and down the staircase, and emergency calls to studios in Calgary and Winnipeg, and the tension of having to decide to move the show in time to make it to another studio in another province, we were all pooped by the time the power returned and the show started, as planned, in Prince Albert.

The current *Cross Country Check-Up* program, with the always entertaining and provocative Rex Murphy, regularly travels to various parts of the country without so much as a missed phone-call. But this trip to Prince Albert was one of the first attempts at a remote broadcast. Premier Blakeney came in and sat down with an aide who was instructed to kick him under the table if the premier got too technical on certain questions. To get out of the line of fire, I tucked my legs under my chair, and we proceeded to chat quite amiably for a few minutes before the start of the show.

I had expressed to the producer my concern that, not having the phones in front of me, I couldn't be sure that the phone call had been properly put through the studio board back in

Montreal. The producer assured me he would give me the okay sign when to go to the first caller. It was an odd sensation doing a phone-in show without a phone in sight, but not nearly as odd as what happened once we began.

Or perhaps I should say, as odd as what happened when I said hello to Premier Blakeney on the air. I heard everything he said, from the moment he opened his mouth, with a seven-second delay. So my eyes and my ears were seeing and hearing two different things. I know, I know, not so odd with a politician ... but in this setting, it was completely unnerving. My ears would tell me to wait until his answer finished, but my eyes were looking at a man whose lips were clearly not moving and a premier who was waiting for the next question.

I'm sure the producer, and the premier for that matter, who were not yet wearing headphones and so were blissfully unaware of what was happening, thought first that I was having a stroke. They finally realized, though, that there was some sort of delay in the loop coming back from CBC in Montreal and as I removed my headphones to ignore the problem, the producer frantically set about to correct it.

Which was perfectly fine, and needed, but he completely forgot that I had no indication if anybody was on the phone ready to take part in the program. So I couldn't just say, as we used to, "*Cross Country Check-Up*, where are you calling from?" or, as we sometimes wanted to say, "*Cross Country Check-Up*, who helped you dial?" and I was left to talk with the premier of Saskatchewan endlessly.

We were almost reduced to talking about the premier's favorite color when the problem was corrected and we proceeded to the phones, about 15 minutes later than usual.

On the way home, we stopped for a few much-needed beers at the airport, forgetting that there had to be food on the table in Saskatchewan before an alcoholic beverage could be served. Actually, we were told one item from the menu for each beer. I'm quite confident we set the record for the number of cheese plates brought to one table in such a short period of time. That was the last time we took *Cross Country* out of our Montreal studio.

"Can cancer be beaten?" was the question of the other *Cross Country Check-Up* program I remember vividly. The first caller was the singer Catherine MacKinnon, who spoke deliberately and passionately from the heart about her sister who was successfully battling the disease. At the time, I remember being impressed that a celebrity like McKinnon had taken the time to phone, but her words and the spirit behind them would come to have a significance I could never have imagined.

When I got home, I made my usual daily call to my oldest sister in Toronto. I would always kid her about not listening to the program. When she told me that night she had just been diagnosed with breast cancer, all the voices of hope and determination from across the country on the radio rang inside my head – without offering much comfort. Like so many other people who suddenly find themselves on the fringes of cancer, I think I was numb for a few days, but then what I had to do became very clear to me.

SIX

THE MEETING

I had to move back to Toronto even though I didn't have a job waiting for me, an act which seems infinitely more foolhardy today than it did then. It was the early '80s and the CBC was still a place which offered options, so I gambled that something would come up. I sold the house in a town called Dewitteville, about an hour drive southwest of Montreal, loaded poor old Moe and Ed back into the car, and headed west once again.

That kind of gamble reminds me of golfer Lee Trevino's response when he was asked once about performing under pressure. He said he never felt it when putting for $165,000 dollars. It only hit him if he had $5 in his pocket and the bet was for $10.

Leaving my job and CBC Montreal and driving off with no prospects was the equivalent for me of putting for $165,000. I can think of at least a couple of reasons now why I should have been more nervous, but then it was one of the clearest decisions I can remember making. I think I've always believed that the heart is as valuable a compass as the head and, while the heart is not always easy to read, I try to look there first for guidance.

So there was no doubt in my heart or my mind that leaving Montreal and Quebec was the right move.

While my sister's illness was the primary motivation, I don't want to leave the impression it was the *only* reason I pulled up stakes. I had pretty much run out of professional options in Montreal. I never had a driving ambition to return to Toronto and was quite content to live and work in what is viewed as the regions, in the CBC context.

It was the *kind* of work rather than the *level* which had me gazing over the fence at, if not greener, at least different pastures.

I left with some sadness. I enjoyed hosting *Cross Country Check-Up* and I wasn't really sure what I wanted or could do next.

The experience of being almost called to a profession so early on is unsettling when that old proverb about the danger of actually getting what you want comes true. I had already done all I had ever expected to do with the CBC five years or so before, on the *Entertainment Section*.

I still feel like I was blessed to be so sure of what I wanted to do at such a young age but, as I'm sure is true for any profession, it means that other options and possibilities are left unexamined – which is fine, if the grip of the initial passion remains firm. But it's frightening when that grip slips, when you wake up one morning and realize the anchor has been unhooked.

But it isn't only a matter of remaining true to the first calling. It seems so easy to fall into a pattern of life which stops questioning, which no longer wants to learn or seek new challenges. One night in Boston I listened to the renowned cellist Yo Yo Ma tell a kind of parable which hit home, and in telling it to you I begin, as he did, by suggesting that the genders can be reversed as necessary.

Every day, the story went, a worker would gather with his colleagues to eat his box lunch which he had brought from home, and every day this one fellow would complain out loud about getting peanut butter sandwiches again.

After weeks of listening to this daily complaint, someone asked the clearly unhappy complainer, "Why don't you ask your wife to make you something different?"

The worker replied, "I'm not married."

I think we all run the risk of becoming so comfortable and so set in our ways that we end up existing more than living. I've been thinking that when we only exist, we're not even aware that we've robbed ourselves of an inner kind of wonder and spirit. It's a theft which extinguishes potential.

So while there were many benefits to my youthful certainty, my increasing professional and spiritual restlessness in middle age has left me dancing with the unexpectedly odd partner of doubt.

Part of my certainty in the early '80s was to get back to Toronto. I figured I could pick up enough fill-in work with CBC to survive and was confident enough in my abilities that something else in radio would come along, sooner or later.

I've hesitated saying this out loud because it always struck me as slightly pathetic when I've heard others express similar sentiments, but here it is. The only place I have any degree of confidence is, in fact, behind a radio microphone. I know what I'm doing there. I just love being in a radio studio. I love the sound of it, the soft felt on the padded table to help muffle noise. I love the heaviness of the door that closes on one world while opening up another. I love having the lights dimmed and reaching out with words.

I keep thinking of C.S. Lewis' comment in *Surprised by Joy* about his mother's family. He wrote that they had a "high talent" for happiness, that they'd go straight for it the way an experienced traveler knows how to grab the best seat on the train. I only share such "high talent" in a radio studio.

I'm not sure how common that situation is or the kind of people in whom it develops. But when it does, you can see how "work" takes on dimensions not generally associated with a "job," i.e., paying the bills and making a living. I have to tell you that nothing in life bores me more than money. I have gone through periods when I've made more than I needed, but also through times, like now, when the wolves aren't only at the door, they're in the living room lifting and labeling furniture.

If you are annoyed by those who say they would have done the work without any pay, you might think of skipping this paragraph. I am one of those people and it is still true today, over 25 years after that first experience behind a microphone, that I have an abiding love for radio, as strong now as ever.

Passion is not easily lived with. I took what I did and how I did it very personally and constantly fought against the cynical aloofness worn like a medal by so many blowhards in the media. These types have perfected a kind of world weariness as they drone on endlessly about truly and profoundly insignificant matters. Their great and only skill is sucking the joy out of everything. I'm not now and never was embarrassed to say that I wanted what I did to mean something.

I know, I know. That sounds horribly pretentious. I suffer from no illusion that everything was critical, but I know this: I never got used to seeing it as a game. I'd cringe when I'd catch myself happy that this or that had gone wrong. We, in the media, depend on human failure or excess and I'm as guilty as the next person in feeling that excitement.

My adrenalin level would jump when I'd hear that Sadat or Gandhi had been gunned down, or that Reagan had been shot. It's awful to say that, but, in every newsroom everywhere in the world, it's the truth – and, I think, a big reason why people are drawn to the profession.

It's a given that journalists live on the misfortune of others, and to pretend otherwise is a silly game played by the uninformed. The only saving grace, for me anyway, lies in how the information is handled and to what purpose you direct your energies.

If you allow it all to become a blur – when a murder over there is the same as the accident over here is the same as crime everywhere – then I think your work reflects a bankruptcy of spirit. When that mindset takes over, and it does very easily, you wake up one morning an adrenalin junkie, left to spend the day chasing cheap thrills but feeling nothing.

I still think, probably from my days in a small town in New Brunswick, that the conversation which takes place once the television or radio is turned off is at least as important as the one just relayed electronically. I would hope there's a practical role for the media to play in people's lives, but that's been kind of lost as its self-importance and extraordinary influence has grown.

A big part of my job, I thought, was to do my best in reducing, if not erasing, the presence of the "medium" from whatever exchange was taking place, and the closer the conversation resembled the one which might take place around a kitchen table, the happier I was with the results.

I was content to sketch the boundaries of a debate, concentrating on and highlighting the gray and infinitely richer areas of any given issue, deliberately resisting the tempting allure of certainty. It was an approach which allowed me to sleep at night, but which set me on a collision course with television, which, while transmitted in color, delivers only black and white.

It's kind of an unexpected role to have carved out for myself – this fireman in the middle of a blaze discussing the merits of smoke alarms. While there were plenty of days I wished I could have stayed at that imaginary kitchen table, I also vigorously embraced this almost "un-media" missionary role to save it from itself. This road to redemption turned out to be much shorter and more pleasant in radio than in television, but, of course, I didn't know that *then*. There was lots I didn't know as *les chats* and I headed out of Quebec.

I had arranged to rent an old farm house north of Toronto, outside the town of Keswick, and I was confident we'd settle in quite comfortably. My furniture would not be arriving until the next day, but my sister had kindly volunteered to come up from the city with an air mattress for me to sleep on, so all seemed arranged and ready.

It was one of those unbelievably close, hot sticky days in southern Ontario, so we were all more than pleased when we peeled ourselves from the car and had a look at our new house. I set out on a tour and, like Martin Balsam climbing the stairs in *Psycho*, the instant I entered the upstairs hallway, my eyes were drawn to the bright red water in the toilet bowl.

I never quite understood why people were so afraid to have a shower after seeing *Psycho*. It seemed to me that transvestites were far scarier than showers. In any case, I gingerly approached the bathroom – waiting for Norman Bates to lunge out at me – and saw a dead bat floating in the toilet.

I noticed that in the old windows of this house, there was a kind of wooden strip at the bottom which had been lifted to let a little air in, considering the oppressive heat. The poor bat must have crawled through and met the Ty-D-Bol® man.

My sister arrived with the emergency supplies and we had a short visit. As a certain slant of darkness fell, Moe and Ed and Emily Dickinson and I were alone. Or so I thought. I sat on the mattress in the living room with a stiff drink in hand and wondered what in the world I was going to do now. Like the grief-stricken at a funeral, I had put so much energy into the move that I hadn't given much thought to what had been lost or what to do next.

All this was swirling around in my head when I suddenly heard the unmistakable flapping sound a bat makes in full flight. I jumped up just in time to almost collide with it as it swooped in from the dining room, through the living room at a height of about six feet, and disappeared around the corner.

I ran from the house and was half-way down the long drive, without the first clue where I was going, before it dawned on me that it would probably be better if Moe and Ed didn't get into a fight with our visitor. So I sheepishly returned to the house, a little embarrassed that my flight response was greater than theirs.

I have always been absolutely terrified of bats and the rest of this hot night was spent running around the house, waving the fireplace baffle – the only weapon available to me – at this poor creature, while Moe and Ed sat there calmly watching the ping pong game. Finally, I'm ashamed to say, I killed the bat, but still slept with one eye open that first night.

With an ease which now surprises me, the "bat house" became a new home and I was picking up work at the CBC , filling in on programs like *As It Happens* and *Morningside*. The work was fulfilling and satisfying and I remained largely on auto-pilot.

This ease, however, which had allowed me to land on my professional feet time and again, was fooling me into thinking that it was only the work which mattered. As long as I kept getting hired, I reasoned, everything was fine. And as long as I believed that, a whole portion of my life, in terms of friendships and family and interests, was left largely ignored.

During this period, I struggled with time off. I remember dreading weekends and holidays because I didn't know what to do with myself. I was so thoroughly consumed by work that its absence actually scared the hell out of me. I think I'm getting a bit closer to where I'd like to be in that personal way today and I hope I have successfully weaned myself from that awful treadmill of earn and spend.

As it was the fall, I asked the landlord to send someone over to check on the old coughing and belching rusted metal monster hulking in the corner of the basement. When the repairman arrived, he said the first thing he had to do was check and perhaps clean the exhaust pipe leading from the furnace through the century-old stone foundation to the chimney.

I followed him down to the basement and through cobwebs worthy of *Indiana Jones* we faced the furnace and its exhaust pipe. He explained – through grunts and groans – how he would simply pull on – more grunts and groans – the pipe to disengage it – just like this – from the foundation.

Suddenly, it broke apart, only to drop a wheelbarrow-sized pile of live snakes onto the dirt floor of the basement.

This wriggling surprise, combined with the recent sightings in the living room of crawling creatures with hard black backs the size of Volkswagen hatchbacks soft-shoeing their way across the top of the couch, made travel plans urgent and easy. The cats and I were out of the bat/snake/beetle house within two weeks.

I had signed a contract to host a medical show on CBC radio, and things seemed to be looking up. Most importantly, it felt like our family had dodged a bullet and would be one of those lucky ones to be only temporarily visited by cancer.

The immediate threat had passed, my sister had made it through the excruciating chemotherapy and surgery, and we all, more or less, resumed our normal routines. For me, that meant filling in for Gzowski on *Morningside*, while I waited for the medicine show to begin.

Tina Srebotnjak was one of the program's experienced producers then, and one morning she mentioned that a still fairly new television program on CBC called *Midday* was looking for a permanent male co-host to work with Valerie Pringle.

I had seen about five minutes of *Midday* when I was still in Montreal and wondered only how Keith Morrison's hair could possibly look so perfect all the time. Other than that brief glimpse, I knew nothing about the program, or Valerie, for that matter.

I had only ventured, with more hesitation than enthusiasm, before the dreaded television camera once before, on a happily-forgotten summer replacement show in Montreal called *Turning Point*. The idea had been a good one, or at least, as so often happens, it *sounded* good in the office.

Once a week, for half an hour, we would interview someone whose life had been redirected at some point by some event. Hence, the rather clever name of *Turning Point*. As it turned out, it should have been subtitled "Tell us about your operation and hospital stay." It was largely an unpleasant experience.

So I went – on a lark, really – to see about the *Midday* job. It was inconceivable to me that I'd land a position on CBC television, especially at the network level, armed with virtually no experience. But I wasn't doing much of anything else, so "Why not?" I thought. Sometimes the simplest questions have the most difficult answers.

The whole experience of the audition was like entering a dark room on a bright sunny afternoon. I knew there were people and things there, but I couldn't quite make them out clearly, and although everyone was very pleasant, I was relieved to get out of there with my radio arrogance intact.

I just couldn't believe it when senior producer Michael Harris actually offered me the job. I remember standing on the sidewalk of Jarvis Street outside the old radio building in downtown Toronto, saying to him, "Surely there's something else you have to ask me about, isn't there?"

He laughed the same way he does when not settling accounts after losing a bet.

"I suppose you want Ramadan off?"

That was it!

I was now Valerie Pringle's co-host on a show I had never seen in a medium I knew nothing about. "Television to call *my* own," I guess.

There was the obligatory haircut and new wardrobe, of course, and as they were paying for both I didn't squabble much. But the process of being led by the hand to a clothing store and then having 12 people, like a jury, in on the decision regarding "His Hair" taught me quickly that the first role of a television host is allowing oneself to become an object.

It's very strange to hear yourself suddenly talked about in the third person, and quite discomfiting to face comments about your hair, your face, your socks, your pants, your weight, your nose, your tie – you name it – from total strangers. It is not an exercise I recommend for the faint of heart.

These things seem like, and in some respects are, just the trivial and minor irritations that come with the territory and even though I think they can be and often *are* taken too seriously, I do believe they are at the top of television's slippery slope. They represent the tiny way that priorities – personal and professional – begin to be stood on end.

I may be wrong about this and take it too seriously – after all, I'm the guy under the apple tree at the perfect summer barbecue party discussing death – but there is a level of mostly benign deception involved in the very act of doing television in a way that just doesn't inherently exist on radio.

The truth about hosting a television show is that, contrary to initial hopes and reasonable expectations, you are in control of almost nothing. A painful example of this was the case of American talk show host Jenny Jones, forced to testify at the murder trial of one of her guests who had killed another one of her guests for what he felt was the public humiliation he suffered as a result of appearing on her program. The specific details of the case don't matter as much as what was revealed, in a general way, when the tip of the iceberg of television deception was exposed.

Ms. Jones was forced to concede that, in fact, she had nothing to do with the selection of topic or guest, that she knew nothing of arrangements made between guest and producer and that essentially she "was only following orders" from the control room during the taping of the show.

Effective but not particularly tough questioning left her wondering aloud in court why she even had a talk show. I watched her with some sympathy. I'll tell you this happens so innocently, the demands of television are so nagging, that you simply come to accept it as a completely normal compromise in the hectic business of getting something on the air.

There were lots of warning signs early on, if I'd been looking for them. One happened when a *Midday* producer had the bright idea to bring together the two previous male hosts – Bill Cameron and Keith Morrison – with me, all of us lined up like crows in a shooting gallery on *Midday*'s couch. The idea was to give Valerie a public chance to say goodbye to them and hello to me. The degree of discomfort I felt then returns even now as I write these words and begin to squirm in my chair.

For someone like me, with no television experience, wearing new, itchy pants, a face full of unusual make-up under an ordered haircut that had me looking like one of those scrubbed and squeaky-clean "Up with People" singers, to suddenly be placed beside the impeccably dressed and coiffed Keith Morrison in front of a television camera, was humbling, to say the least.

I remember looking down at my feet at one point in that conversation and noticing that I had different colored socks on. I couldn't believe it. Although I asked Keith if he would leave his hair for me, the other question rattling around my brain was what in the world was I doing on this couch with these people?

One thing it turned out I was doing was becoming better known and recognized. It might seem silly to point that out, but you have no idea what that was like for me after so many virtually anonymous years with CBC radio. I liked it, sort of.

But "television attention" is odd and feels like it has something to do with the field of semiotics, as proposed over 100 years ago by the American scientist and logician Charles Pierce.

I don't pretend to any expertise, but understand that what he called "semiotics" is about the science and power of symbols.

This goes some way toward explaining how men who look more like Karl Malden can paint on sideburns and put on a jump suit and make you think of Elvis Presley. There's a similar disconnection which takes place when someone knows your image or "symbol" only through a television set.

To be the recipient of such recognition is, at first, quite unsettling, but the more often it happens, the more it becomes normal and just part of a new mask to be worn. I have been mistaken for Peter Mansbridge, which might conceivably be explained by our common first names. But someone with whom I had been having a reasonable conversation once asked if I was Lloyd Robertson!

The reasons behind that attention are interesting to me. Simply appearing on television separates you from the viewer in a way that speaking to a listener through a radio microphone doesn't. It is impossible in television, at least it was for me, not to begin to feel separate, certainly from the audience, but also disconnected from yourself in some important ways.

Consider. There are people to wash and comb your hair every day, people to cover up last night's party in your eyes, people to make sure your clothing is right, people to run your lines through a contraption you read from under the camera lens, people to cover up sweat, people in the ceiling controlling lights to make you look better – if they're on your side. Essentially, all you have to do is show up and be prepared to wait. And you make a lot of money to be pampered like this.

Even the language used within the business is revealing. On most days, hosts are further removed from reality by being referred to as "the talent." Allow me to use it in a sentence for you. "Where the _ _ _ _ is the talent? Get them on set." And that's only the command I actually *heard*.

This is one of the fundamental reasons why television is the perfect medium for people who crave attention. There are always others running around to make things right for you. You are set apart from and usually above the crowd because of the money, and if you're comfortable being larger than life, you love that distinction.

To this day, I feel considerably *smaller* than life and so it took an enormous amount of confidence I didn't really have, to "perform" in public like that. The best description of this discomfort I heard was from someone who, like me, left a great job in television in Toronto. She said the problem for her was that in addition to getting the story or interview right, which is hard enough and is all that should matter, there was the daily pressure to "put on a show."

All I'm sure of is that I could never have done it if it hadn't been for the wonderful production people who surrounded *Midday* at that time. Like my start at CBC in Fredericton, I was blessed to work with colleagues who were helpful, patient and supportive.

Director Sidney Cohen and floor director Rene Dowhaniuk were the two I worked most closely with on the simple mechanics of television. They did their best to prevent me from looking like a deer caught in the headlights of a car during those first weeks. I think, somehow, they mostly succeeded.

But the person who made me feel most at home was Valerie Pringle. I'm aware that much has been whispered about our eventual "break-up," and it's taken both of us some time to gain a little perspective on it all. We couldn't hold more different life views and it's true that we were driving each other crazy by the end of our time together. I accept most of the responsibility for that.

I'll tell you what I've told her recently: if the chance to work with Valerie ever came along again, I would grab it with no questions asked. Well, almost none. She welcomed me to that *Midday* desk in small but gentle ways no one else would ever notice. She almost literally held my hand through those first days in television and was more generous than she had to be. I was grateful and grew more and more fond of her.

You wouldn't believe me if I told you what a ball we had together in the beginning. When we weren't working, and sometimes when we were, we'd spend most of our time laughing with each other. I remember once, as we prepared to host the Easter Seal Telethon in Toronto and we were going on about something and giggling, a veteran floor director came over shaking his head and said, "God, it is true about you two."

One of the first fundamental things I think Valerie and I shared, which initially cemented our friendship, was a sense that, after all, this is *only* a television program. It may seem like a small philosophy to hold two people together, but believe me, it is rare in this strange television world overflowing with its own self-importance and peacock-strutting egos. And it doesn't endear one to those who take it so seriously.

I slowly but happily surrendered to the demands of television. I always noticed how distracted visiting guests would become by the scurrying around that goes on behind the camera, and I think Valerie and I shared a desire not to take it all very seriously.

It strikes me that hosting television is like swinging a golf club. As long as your head is empty, you'll knock the ball a mile. Once you start concentrating on how it's done, you're lucky to get it off the tee. And so there were situations in television which you learned simply to look beyond. For example, it is not normal to interview someone you pretend to see when, in fact, you're staring at a blank wall. We'd do that every day, sometimes with pretty funny results.

We would routinely ask the guest – who couldn't see us either, by the way – to describe what was behind them, but they weren't always honest. We did an interview with striking nurses in Alberta one day and were assured they were just sitting in an office, with nothing special around them. When the tape came in there was a blackboard behind them with the clearly legible scribbled sentence, "the only good Tory is a suppository." Some fast editing was done to spare the country the delicacies of Alberta politics.

For some reason, I remember the exact moment I felt like the transformation had been completed and that this person who valued word and thought on radio had now completely succumbed to the odd world of television and *Midday*.

The poet Irving Layton was the guest and we had a fairly amiable chat at the desk which ended with his passionate recitation of a powerful poem about the suicide of a relative. It's curious, and I think worth further thought, how television seems to demand the trivialization of such riveting moments. I obliged by immediately asking if he thought the Blue Jays would win the World Series that year.

If Layton hadn't exploded in laughter, my fledgling television career might have ended then and there, but he did. And I went home that day knowing, without much pride and only a little shame, that I had just done my first "real" television interview.

SEVEN

THE SEDUCTION

It's quite a journey to go from believing in the possibilities and great promise of television to reaching the conclusion that it is the single greatest polluter in the world, but that's the unexpected trip I've taken. Pico Iyer, in his wonderful, insightful book *Video Night in Katmandu*, writes of the disappointment many Westerners feel when they travel to the East and vice versa. He points out that many of us from the West go with the hope of discovering some ancient wisdom which will transform and fill with meaning our North American lives which feel increasingly empty.

The image those in the East have of Westerners, Iyer writes, is largely from movies and television, and so their expectation is that we're all fabulously wealthy, we live in Beverly Hills, and, when we're not making another million, we're lounging in our backyard swimming pools. This is clearly a recipe cooked up in the media "kitchen," resulting in a meal of mutual disappointment all around.

It's astonishing to witness television's reach and that's what makes some uneasy with the way it's being used. I remembered Iyer's words in Bangladesh, when I saw children running on the beach wearing *McGyver* t-shirts from the television series. A few years before, at the Romanian-Hungarian border just after the Ceausescus were murdered, our entry was delayed because the Romanian guards were watching reruns of *Dallas*.

Even had I been aware of it, I don't know what I could have done to have prevented television from feeding my vanity while starving my self-respect. How that begins to happen, innocently enough and through no one's fault or malicious intent, is a measure of the desire which surrounds a television camera, the almost magnetic force which draws people to be behind or in front of it.

I was always a bit troubled by people's hunger to get in front of that camera, and amazed by what they were willing to put up with to get there. There are two kinds of people in this regard: those who know exactly how television operates and those who don't have a clue.

The former, for whom I felt more suspicion than worry, knew how to look after themselves. But the latter always appeared to me to be like lambs, submissively exposing their tiny necks in the great abattoir of television. It was never a fair fight and I found myself, again and again, taking their side against mine.

We once went to visit the late, distinguished diarist and diplomat Charles Ritchie in Ottawa. You should know that in those days of healthier budgets, "we," in CBC television terms, meant a host, a producer, a cameraman and a soundman. Our arrival anywhere was more of an invasion than a visit and although I'm sure the experienced Mr. Ritchie knew something about the process, he was still unready for what happened.

The cameraman, as interior designer, would quickly assess the location and then set about to correct it. Windows offering natural light were covered with heavy black cloth, which hung like funereal drapes, and furniture was moved around at will.

The soundman would cock his head to one side like a retriever and declare that the refrigerator, two floors and seven rooms away, was making such a racket that it absolutely had to be unplugged.

Anything else that might hum, hiss, or squeak indicating that we were actually somewhere with real noises was also summarily shut off. You can imagine how popular this practice made us when we visited offices in the sweltering heat of August and "Radar" the soundman would insist the air conditioning be turned off.

I never understood why we were so deathly afraid of those real and everyday noises. I suppose it might be just another attempt television makes to create its own world by silencing the one we all live in. I lost track of the number of times an interview was stopped because a plane flew overhead or a truck went by the window.

The worst case ever was a situation in Los Angeles when I had the temerity to do a difficult interview in, of all places, the outdoors. From the corner of my eye, I could see the soundman twisting his head around like he'd been possessed by Linda Blair.

The guest was sharing a difficult part of her life with us and all I could do was pray the soundman would remain silent and live with the noises of a city.

The prayer went unanswered. He with the miraculous ears stopped everything because he heard someone bouncing a basketball four streets over in another neighborhood. We had quite a healthy disagreement, in front of the guest no less, about how unusual, really, the sound of a basketball was in the city of Los Angeles.

As best as I was able to discern, the reasoning seems to be that when you're sitting at home watching television you sink into such a trance of stupidity that you're unable to recognize the sound of a plane or a truck if you don't actually see a plane or a truck.

As you might already have guessed, this used to drive me absolutely crazy, only partly because I saw it as surrendering to the technology. Television – at least the kind I was involved with – seemed utterly incapable of spontaneity and was hell-bent on celebrating the obvious while dismissing anything even remotely subtle.

Once television became intellectually handcuffed to the lowest common denominator, the audience would be seen forevermore as a bunch of zombie-like dolts. I never lost faith, though, that there is a great hunger for television that matters.

Returning to my story, the impeccably-dressed and charming Charles Ritchie sat quietly observing the redecoration project underway in his lovely apartment on this afternoon. Just as we were about to finally, at long last, begin the interview, he leaned over to me and in almost a whisper, very politely inquired, "What have you done with my wife?"

I replied that I wasn't sure, but I thought I had seen her escape just as the second bookcase was being moved.

This concern with controlling the environment in which it operates may have begun in response to the particular demands of its hardware, but I think it has now been allowed to take over editorially and is part of television's determination to *create* and not *reflect* reality.

I found myself more and more colliding with that very basic philosophical underpinning of the medium where I now made my living. The once cumbersome technology no longer needs to limit television's possibilities. We live in a time when broadcast quality tape can be delivered by a hand-held camera, but the "thinking" behind the programming has yet to catch up.

Although *Midday* was based largely in a studio and consequently enjoyed almost total control of its environment, I soon learned there were other small steps to be taken on this pleasant path of deception. What's shocking is the speed with which these parts of the television process become normal. Let me give you one small example.

You probably already know that when you see an interviewer asking questions of someone projected on a large screen, generally the interviewer can't actually see the person he or she is talking to, and that the guest is equally blind.

Add to that the fact that the questions you see and hear being asked, in the vast majority of interviews, are rarely the way they were asked the first time around. Trust me, they are made better – meaning shorter and snappier – and they are now phrased and presented to the guest and to you with the questioner enjoying the enormous advantage of knowing how they've already been answered.

When it comes to who's going to look smarter and better and more aggressive – the guest or the host – guess who wins? It was not unusual for experienced guests to demand that the conversation take place live, eliminating the possibility of any tampering.

This routine practice of changing the very nature of a conversation is one of those aspects of television work which truly appalled me at first, but one which just as quickly became part of the job. Not only can you change the tone of the question to your advantage, there are times you ask the questions without the guest even being there anymore. Here's how it works.

We – cameraman, producer, soundman and host – all arrive at your house for the interview. We tell you it'll take about an hour. After an hour and a half setting up, we tell you it's going to only be a few more minutes.

Thirty minutes after that and ten minutes before you've got to leave for that important doctor's appointment we assured you that you wouldn't miss, you and I finally sit down close to one another and have the microphones attached.

You are now electronically connected and are warned that if you have to get up for any reason, be sure to tell us first and the soundman will unhook you. How are you enjoying the experience so far?

You'll probably see hand signals and gestures exchanged between the producer, cameraman and soundman while listening to me make idiotic small talk about relaxing and remembering that this will all be over soon.

At this point, there's a huddle behind us as the producer is invited to look through the camera lens which, if you haven't noticed yet, is pointed directly at you.

"Do you have another sweater you could wear," the producer asks politely, "and if you have a hair brush handy, that would be great." You are filled with confidence.

The producer will spend some more time staring through the lens and then come over and stare, with equal determination from a distance of about three inches, at something on your forehead. But just relax, we'll be ready soon and again, we're very sorry about your doctor's appointment.

"Now," the producer announces, "if you'd just look directly at Peter and please don't say anything. He's going to talk to you."

While recognizing the need for this, I hated rambling on endlessly about the most inane things you could imagine just so we could get a couple of shots of you listening.

"For editing purposes, you see," offers the producer.

You don't, but just relax while I drone on.

"No, no, no," instructs the producer. "Don't smile, don't laugh, don't make a sound. Please, just look at Peter and listen without any expression on your face."

Okay, we're just about ready to start that interview we came here for. But just a second. The cameraman has noticed that the door knob behind you appears to be growing from the top of your head.

Another hurried huddle.

"Could I ask you to please take your glasses off? We're having a reflection problem," explains the producer....

"Yes, I understand, but you don't really have to see, do you?"

You hear your increasingly feeble answers as the tentacles of the television octopus increasingly secure their grip.

"We'll just fix this door knob problem," the cheery producer tells you to the grunts of the crew, "and then we'll be underway. Are you comfortable?"

Before you can answer, the producer says, "Good. Remember, just relax and look at Peter."

"Well," she continues, "it looks like we're going to move into another room because we can't seem to lose that door knob, but you know what, we are losing the light in this room so it'll be much better if we go through to the kitchen with its bigger windows. It'll just take a couple of minutes."

I sit there sheepishly, unable to help you or speed up this process. As I ask if there's anything we could get you, the phone rings and you react normally.

"No! No! No!" shouts the soundman sitting on the floor. Don't stand up, you'll yank the microphone from your clothing. Here we go. We'll take it off. There we are. Now you can get up. By the way, could you unplug that phone when you're finished there? We're almost ready to begin once we get set up in the kitchen."

When you return, the producer explains that we have to get those shots of you listening again now that we're in a different room.

"You're a pro at this now," she says, aware that flattery beats impatience, "so just relax and look at Peter without smiling, nodding, chuckling, or making any kind of face. We just want you to listen. Peter?"

"Well, then I left CJCJ in Woodstock and went to Toronto to work on a program blah, blah, blah, blah, blah..."

"Okay," the producer says triumphantly. "I think we're ready to begin."

She adds quickly, "We better hurry though, the sun's going down."

We finally get around to having a conversation with the camera still only on you. We get a few minutes done until somebody's battery dies. There's a discussion about how it could have possibly died that quickly and whether there's another one in the truck and then your kids come home and are told to be absolutely silent, the cat has heard the kids and is investigating the activity in the kitchen, the battery's replaced and the conversation resumes, and then boom! – just like that, we're running out of time.

When you and I finish talking, you mistakenly believe you're about to be free of us. The relief and smile are extinguished as the producer reenters the picture.

"We're going to turn the camera around," she announces, "and Peter will ask the questions again." She continues as your heart sinks. "It would be great if you could just begin to answer them or move your head so it *looks* like you're really talking. It'll just take a moment to get set up."

At this stage of the process as the camera is moved behind you, "really talking" means the back of your head moving up and down or from side to side, but believe it or not, we are still some time away from getting to that.

"I guess we're going to need lights now that it's getting darker. It'll just be a while."

"Sure," the soundman pipes in, "you can go see your kids. Let me unhook you. I'll get your glasses for you. There you are. We'll call when we're ready."

In 30 minutes when we call you again, we've now been in your house for four and a half hours. We've unplugged your phone and your fridge, we've moved furniture, silenced your children, and angered the cat. You've missed your doctor's appointment, but it's all worth it, isn't it?

What you may not have noticed, as we were having our conversation, was the furious scribbling which engaged the producer. My questions are recorded as accurately as possible as they are asked. Once we move the camera around so it is now positioned looking over your shoulder directly at me, the producer reads the questions back and I repeat them as if we had had two cameras during the initial conversation. Still with me?

Once the two tapes are in the editing suite they can be "married" to an almost lifelike resemblance of a normal conversation. It looks like the answer follows the question which follows the answer. Wonderful technology.

But as you can guess by now, this elaborate process results in the furthest thing from a normal conversation. Any cross-talk, any emotion, any element of a passionate exchange is virtually lost to the demands of the editor. The stark choice facing the host at this point is to be an interviewer or an actor. Once the two are combined, there's rarely a genuine exchange between the two of us which makes it to air.

When I was still in radio, I wondered why Gzowski had insisted on having two cameras in a later television show of his, but once I slapped on the make-up and spent a few months doing these re-asks, as they're called, I quickly learned why. I got the hang of it, but was still uncomfortable acting, so I started to edit the conversations as we went along to make my job easier and less embarrassing.

A small example. I always dreaded the possibility that the guest might make me laugh, which you should know is not very difficult. I learned I would have to laugh again as naturally and easily as the original, once the camera was moved around. This is the real talent of a television interviewer or at least the one most valued by the producers and editors who must make the program. Again, the demands of television's machinery dictate the boundaries of everything on it.

As if that weren't enough, I discovered there are times when the guest has to leave and the questions are repeated to either an empty chair or a member of the crew. The empty chair scenario can create problems with the eye line between the two of us, so often a member of the crew is more than happy to sit in, with mixed results.

I recall the actress Sally Field, who was exhausted after a day of interviews, having to leave the instant her part of the interview had ended. The producer, who was a swarthy-looking, mustachioed Moroccan with a heavy beard, replaced Sally when it came time for the re-asks.

I started to get the giggles, searching this man's dark eyes, asking him about "the time you spent as the Flying Nun" or what it was like to have played "Norma Rae." By the time we salvaged a few usable re-asks more than an hour later, we were all exhausted and helpless with laughter.

As the answer of the guest in this re-ask situation is rarely used, they can say anything as long as the back of their head moves in a way that suggests they're responding. Ninety-nine per cent of the time, the guest simply offers a shorter version of their original answer, but sometimes, if they're comfortable with the process, they know they can say absolutely anything in response to the repeated questions.

One of the memorable sessions I had with this was with someone who could make me laugh without saying a word. I'll never forget, it was the day the Challenger spacecraft exploded when I went to interview comedian Bob Newhart at his hotel in Toronto.

I was surprised when, without any of the usual entourage, he answered the door to his room himself. The crew hadn't arrived yet and so Newhart and I sat alone watching the television reports of the Challenger tragedy. It was the first and last time I ever remember hoping the crew would be delayed even longer than usual.

Unfortunately, they showed up and we went about the business of doing the interview. But when the camera was moved to get the re-asks, the genuinely funny Newhart started changing all his answers, trying to prevent me, with great success, from asking a question without looking like I was about to burst.

I remember asking him about what it was like to work with Dick Martin – from the old Rowan and Martin comedy team –

who was directing many of the episodes of Newhart's television show at the time. When the camera was on Newhart, he praised Martin's comedic timing and great sense of humor and explained how important and rare those qualities were in a television director.

But it was a different story when the camera was on me. Knowing that this was one exchange we'd use for sure on *Midday*, I asked confidently, "What difference has it made to you to have someone of the calibre of Dick Martin to direct the television show?"

"None," Newhart now responded with that famous deadpan delivery.

My eyes pleaded, "Please don't do this to me."

"I've never understood why anyone ever thought Dick was funny in the first place," Newhart continued, "it's been hell having to work with him."

By this time, everyone in the room was bent over laughing and we struggled to get a little quiet to ask another question. Newhart and I had spoken about the importance of writing in situation comedies and he again was very generous towards his talented writing team.

"It seems that you've always been very careful about the writing on your various television series. How do you manage to keep the quality so high? "

"I do it all myself," Newhart began. "I've never needed writers ..."

And so his answers continued. Then, as if we needed anything else, a new wrinkle was added to the mix. The fire alarm of the hotel started to go on and off randomly, which simply served his wicked sense of humor as he took increasing delight in making my job impossible.

If, by a miracle, I managed to get a question out with neither laughter nor the fire alarm ruining it, it was almost guaranteed to ring at the beginning of his answer. This happened so many times and his mind is so quick, he began incorporating the alarm into his answers. We were now both laughing so hard we couldn't really continue. It was one of my favorite afternoons in television.

There can be other problems with this silly re-ask situation when the guest doesn't actually leave the location but just gets out of the chair.

We sat once by the ocean with Haida carver Bill Reid during Expo in Vancouver. He was having a bad day with his Parkinson's and needed to stand up and stretch while we were doing the re-asks. The problem was, and the producer only noticed this when we were almost done with the bloody things, that Mr. Reid had positioned himself directly behind me and could be clearly seen leaning over the fence staring at the water!

This, of course, meant that when the interview was assembled, it would appear that Mr. Reid would be sitting in a relaxed way talking with me and then suddenly he would be behind me during the questions. Abandoning our initial thought of introducing his previously undiscovered exact twin to a national television audience, we began the re-asks again.

Sometimes the elements would cause us grief. On the same trip to Expo, I met broadcaster Jack Webster and the late journalist Marjorie Nichols. By the time the guest part of the two interviews were finished, the clouds had rumbled in, meaning we couldn't do the re-asks right away.

I'm aware the weather changes quickly on the coast, but even on TV where so little *is* as it seems, it was a bit of a problem to have all the answers delivered in bright sunshine and the questions asked in relative darkness. In an Enneagram kind of way, it was probably a bang-on reflection of the temperaments involved, but that was of precious little use to us as we scrambled to prepare the next day's program.

We had a million other things to do that day so we bade Nichols and Webster farewell and, for the life of me, I couldn't figure out how we were going to make interviews out of the morning's work. It was a good six hours later, in an entirely different location on the Expo site, when I sat down all by myself in the returning sunshine to finish my conversations with Jack and Marjorie.

The major concern at the time was not that what we were doing was fundamentally dishonest, it was only that the scene behind me was compatible with what had been behind Marjorie and Jack in the morning. And you know what? When those interviews aired on *Midday*, even I could have sworn it had happened just the way it looked.

I experienced a strange and not altogether pleasant feeling at the sight of this. Being the new guy and having entered a world where this kind of deception was apparently commonplace, I felt an almost illicit pride in a sense of collusion, of successfully making my first hit tying me inextricably forevermore to television's version of the Mob. My desire to belong and to be accepted was stronger than the whispers from my conscience.

But I *knew* that it was – well, forgive me the language, but it was bullshit. Although, I reassured myself, this was clearly a fairly benign act on the part of mainly good-willed people, I began to understand how malleable television's truth was, and how convincing were its lies.

Years later, a producer on *Man Alive*, with its remarkable reputation for thoughtful programming, actually suggested without a trace of shame or conscience that a cut-away be shot of me and used in an interview I had never been a part of.

You may know this, but whenever you see a shot of the television interviewer listening, it's the spot of an edit. This particular producer saw me as an obstacle and went ahead on her own whenever she got the chance. But now she was stuck with an awkward edit and no cut-away.

Even more alarming to me was that she saw nothing wrong with her proposed solution to accomplish the edit she otherwise couldn't achieve. I knew enough by then to say no. But the more I learned, the more uneasy I became.

What mattered above everything else, obviously, was that you had material to present and, given television's constant and voracious appetite for more product, it was all you could do to keep up with the demand. If that meant a few corners cut here and there from such a labor intensive exercise, so what?

As the result of early experiences like this, I was beginning to feel distanced from my work in a way that I never felt on radio. There are no corners to cut when it's simply you, the guest, and a microphone. The images can only flow from imagination, which in turn can only function when engaged, so as a radio interviewer, a part of me was a part of each conversation. I *was* an interviewer on radio, but only *played* one on television.

Having said that, I knew at the same time that I was being seduced by television's frightening power. I felt myself being almost hypnotically drawn to its glow, enjoying the attention it brought and the influence it promised. Television plays a unique kind of tune to which everyone seems eager to dance. And as the caller at that dance, you just feel pretty important. Period. It is that simple.

Apart from the *conversations* which can be mangled in television's teeth, *images* can also be chewed over and spat out to look like whatever is needed. Valerie and I did a few *Midday* programs sitting atop Scotchman's Hill overlooking Calgary during the '88 Winter Olympics. It's a choice spot with a great view of the city as a backdrop, but when we first went to the location, the ground was covered with what looked like millions of those small pieces of styrofoam packing material.

It was explained that when the American network holding Olympic rights had come to do their promotional ads for their upcoming coverage, it hadn't looked "wintry" enough. It wasn't bad enough that they'd brought in truckloads of this Styrofoam snow, they also hadn't lifted a finger to clean up.

This is the medium which so largely defines our society and informs our culture and yet it is one which displays no inclination to reflect what actually is. It goes out into the world with a notion of how it should be and proceeds to create this image. And it doesn't take a rocket scientist to see who says what "should be."

Television has become the oil in today's massive corporate engine and, consequently, isn't the slightest bit interested in questioning the status quo. Advertisers' demands march in lock step with the corporate agenda to ensure that the powerless and the weakest in our community will never have a voice in today's most powerful chorus. For those who *feel*, that silence is as troubling as it is deafening.

Television still held some surprises and there was much I had to learn, but even at this early stage I found myself increasingly concerned about and drawn to those who weren't being represented.

EIGHT

THE STRUGGLES

The more I worked in and learned about television, the less I came to respect it and myself, a requirement which was becoming increasingly important to me. I tried to figure out what quality my friends who still managed to work in television had that I didn't. It's not as if they feel they're wasting their time in a medium which demands so much of it. But it wasn't for me and my impatience with the process was growing.

Every day spent waiting for some part of its machinery to work was an exercise in supreme frustration. I eventually raised the white flag and surrendered, concluding that life was too short to spend waiting around for a light to be fixed or for a cloud to roll by. More seriously, I was coming to embrace the idea that what is essential in life is mostly invisible – a somewhat awkward philosophy when one makes one's living in television.

More and more I became aware that the medium truly values only surface qualities. And I mean that beyond simply the physical. By now, that aspect of the exercise was routine. Not only was I asking for and wearing mascara and hair spray five out of seven days, but I now even knew what shades of make-up I was supposed to wear. "Gay Whisper," if you must know.

What I mean by surface values is that while television is undoubtedly a very good recorder of our times, it is far less effective when it comes to interpreting the meaning behind events. Just as the personal video camera has changed how and what we as individuals record and value, I think the television camera continues to fundamentally distort the lens through which we see our life and times.

As an example, the camera can show the world the exhilaration and joy surrounding the destruction of the Berlin Wall, but unlike radio, for example, it can't get into the kitchens and living rooms of ordinary Germans to explore the fears and worries bubbling just beneath the surface of this event.

I mean, obviously, it *can*, physically, get into those places, but it's just so cumbersome and intrusive that it changes everything in front of it. The camera becomes an obstacle between people and magically bestows upon the one who owns it an authority, whether warranted or not.

And it's all packaged in such a way that everyone is polished and well-dressed, and articulate with quick answers, a handy solution, or wise advice to offer. The camera craves black and white certainty and shuns life's pauses or moments of doubt. I don't know about your life, but mine has more moments of doubt than certainty.

So for someone like me, whose professional and personal life were inextricably linked, whose work was never a job in the traditional sense, it's not exactly a bulletin that television wasn't equipped for the larger personal task I placed before it.

Nor did I seem capable of adjusting to its demands. I can hardly blame it for only being what it is. It's just that it was becoming more urgent that I try to discover what *I* was.

But all was not lost. In the same way one good golf shot out of 100 bad ones can have you returning to the course with the fresh optimism of a new day, television could deliver a tempting morsel that would have me believing again in its promise.

The temptation was strong enough that I was still hauling myself out of bed at precisely 4:43 a.m. each morning so that I could get to the Toronto studios in time to look over that day's material, get made up, and do the show with Valerie to the Maritimes live at 11:00 a.m. eastern.

I think it was a pretty good show, too. We tried our best to represent all parts of the country and part of that goal was accomplished, I think, by putting people on who would otherwise have never been visited by television. You'll have to ask them if they thought the experience was worth it, but it certainly was for us.

This desire to be as "Un-Toronto" as possible is an oft-repeated promise made by national broadcasters, and it is much easier to say than to achieve. The major obstacle is that a clear and committed vision is required at the top of the program structure to inform every part of the program with this mandate. It doesn't and can't happen by accident.

Our compass on *Midday* was Suzanne Boyce, who set us on a course which, as far as I can see, hasn't been followed by any other Canadian television show. I'd like to think that Suzanne is a friend, despite our beginning and ending at *Midday*.

In the same way a person without sight checks the position of furniture in an unfamiliar room, I always had to "feel" my way around new authority. That process resulted in a memorable meeting early on, when I accused Suzanne of being like Brian Mulroney, of not having a larger vision for the program. I was as wrong about her as most Canadians were about him. It's just that she had a little trouble sharing her vision out loud.

Among the less public but more important signals that the CBC is in real, real trouble, is the fact that it can't accommodate gifted senior management like Suzanne Boyce, whose immense abilities now serve Baton Broadcasting.

When we were all together at *Midday*, she was the heart and soul of the program, even as we used to good-naturedly kid her all the time about her shyness and her tendency to mumble her way through meetings. She created, with great skill and care, an atmosphere in which many dedicated people across the country put in impossibly long hours.

Of course, in the real world, it shouldn't take so much work to allow someone in a studio in Toronto to speak with a lobster fisherman in his boat off the coast of Prince Edward Island. But in the netherworld of television, it does. The only way people will do all that work is if they feel like they're a valued and worthwhile part of something. Suzanne made us all – even me – believe that "*Midday* Works," as she was fond of saying, and as she eventually put on a button.

Suzanne is from Saint John, New Brunswick, and has that kind of instinctive feel for the modesty and sensibility of the Canadian character. "Respect" sounds like too fussy a word to describe the personal quality that's needed to celebrate the parts and people of this country on a daily show. It has to be under your skin and part of who you are to understand that Toronto is not Canada.

You can be sure the conventional wisdom which says the television camera never lies was started by television people trying to reassure themselves. Nonetheless, it is true that it occasionally reveals the truth. In my experience, for example, it doesn't allow you to *pretend* to be interested in the berry-picking family from Newfoundland or the farmer with colored eggs in Nova Scotia. And once caught, recovery is difficult.

Valerie and I continued to share a healthy skepticism about the medium and the strutting self-importance of television types, and I think we both genuinely wanted a program which honored who and what we were as Canadians.

All of us at *Midday*, come to think of it, weren't the slightest bit interested in doing a knock-off of an American talk show and, looking back, I see how – thanks largely to Boyce – we were allowed to revel in our "Canadian-ness."

There's no better example of that than the programs we devoted to deciphering the controversial Free Trade Agreement with the United States. To this day, there are parts of that sell-out agreement which have even the brightest legal minds disagreeing, but for us at *Midday*, it was a more profound question of who we were as a people and what kind of society we wished to have.

I think that's simply something you either get or you don't get, and excuse my bias and immodesty, but I think *Midday* "got it."

For a good while, I loved the job, and I loved working with Valerie. We had a great studio crew and a dedicated bunch of producers. It sounds trite, but *Midday* felt like a family, with all the joys and problems and rewards that come with that designation. On the very best days, it felt to me like we were doing a kind of *Morningside* on television, only it was a million times more difficult.

In radio, you can pick up the phone and, in less than five minutes, unite voices from Aklavik to Campbell River to Plaster Rock to Cape Tormentine. It would cost four crews, travel time, satellite expense, producer's time and on and on to pull something like that off on television.

So to be fair about it, it's not always a lack of intention or desire in television when the time, energy and money involved is so prohibitive.

Without those crews working behind the scenes with us in various parts of the country, we would have been just another Toronto television program, no matter how much we may have wanted to be something more. This is one of the more hidden consequences of the budget cuts. I think CBC management made a fatal strategic error and lost valuable public support in not responding to the cuts by canceling particular programs. Their decision to carry on the programs with slashed budgets has led to continued and mostly hidden internal bleeding, and a slower, more painful and relatively unnoticed death.

Again, the proud and hard-working program people on the front lines, who are there because they believe in public broadcasting, are paying the immediate price for these cuts. Comfortably overpaid managers and ossified producers sit and lament their troubles while others are forced to work through and around their fumbling mistakes.

All of which makes *Midday*'s broadcast from the North that much more incredible, if only for the technical challenges it presented. Just as we never know when we take it which old photograph has captured the essence of someone once they're gone, this broadcast from Inuvik has become the high point of my time with Valerie and the show.

It served partly as a reminder of television's reach, but also confirmed everything we all wanted the program to be. At the heart of that purpose was introducing Canadians to Canadians. And sometimes, when it worked, it was electrifying.

We visited two women – Mona and Annie – and shopped at their small craft store in Tuktoyaktuk. It became one of those remarkable moments when you understand just how incredibly diverse and rich we are as a nation. And how opportunistic.

I think the taxi ride from the airstrip to their store might have been a mile and a half, but quickly spotting a bunch with no other options, we were forced to pay a fortune to the driver who didn't blink when stating his exaggerated price.

Mona and Annie also understood, in a delightfully understated way, the impact of our visit. When asked how business was, they responded, with a twinkle in their eye, "Pretty good now."

As we sat there in this little cabin, surrounded by what seemed to those of us from the south as almost a different, dangerous and frozen planet, the laughter with Mona and Annie made the North become real in a way that touched my heart as a Canadian.

The experience changed my view of who we are and of what we have as a people, and of how much our perceptions of this land flow only from southern eyes. *This* Canada we were visiting was rarely presented on television.

On another level, I learned to be careful about the bets I sometimes made. When Valerie was, I think, seven months pregnant, I stupidly challenged her to a game of squash. She won. Handily. And she talked about it. A lot.

When we stepped off the plane in Tuktoyaktuk, the woman at the airstrip was anxious and pleased to tell us – me, actually – that I was safe. There were no squash courts there.

I don't think I've ever laughed as hard as I did when Valerie and I took off in a helicopter, leaving director Sidney Cohen all alone on the frozen Mackenzie Delta. I can see him still to this day, slowly engulfed in the blinding snow whipped up by the helicopter blades as we disappeared into the gray, snow-filled sky.

Sidney, you should know, is the kind of person who becomes nervous when taken more than 50 feet from a microwave oven and street lights, so his plight, all alone in this vast, cold wilderness, forced tears of laughter to run down our cheeks.

When we returned, only minutes later, to once again bury this by now whimpering mass of suburbia with swirling snow, my favorite moment with Valerie happened spontaneously. We decided this was the spot to do the close to the show. Nothing elaborate. We were going to say goodbye, then turn and walk off into the snow.

We were wearing huge and heavy boots, not to mention an assortment of dead animals to keep us warm, when we headed off into what turned out to be the deep end of the pool. We were slowly but surely being pulled further and further down by the increasingly deep snow. We both tired and ended up falling on our backs.

Although it's not visible, I think the image is clear that we were both laughing in a way that spoke of a real happiness between us, and in those seconds, like that old family photograph which takes on an unexpected importance, the scene captured for me the essence of the time Valerie and I had spent together and with the *Midday* audience. I wish it could have lasted. When I think about those days now I'm proud and grateful that I had the chance to be a part of it.

But, in the process, I was becoming more and more suspicious of television's "theatrical" nature. Not only did "re-asks" now seem quite normal to me, I was introduced to the idea of so-called "double-enders."

This is when only the guest has a crew with him or her and she or he would hear the questions from me through a simple phone line. This means I could be at home in my birthday suit doing the interview, which rarely happened. I always tried, at least, to put on a dressing gown.

When the process is finished, the guest tape would only have the answers, with the blank spaces left for the questions. By rolling that tape, I could now, dressed and on camera in studio, ask the same questions again for exactly the same number of seconds and recorded on yet another tape. And presto, you have something which looks like a perfectly normal conversation that works, but didn't quite happen the way it looks.

A great deal of time was spent in studio perfecting this marriage of question and answer. You can imagine the complications. If you laughed originally, you had to laugh again, but this time for exactly the same number of seconds and at something which might have only been funny the first time around.

If you were emotional about something, that too had to be recreated the next morning to fit in the precise "hole" left in the guest tape, which rolls along waiting for the inserts.

If that hasn't confused you completely, you're better at this than I was at first. While the initial interview might even have a few elements of a journalistic dialogue, the packaging was acting, pure and simple.

Again, after a while, the peculiar demands of television began to wear me down and started to change the way I would conduct interviews, if only to make it easier on all of us in the studio the next morning.

The stop and start nature of this could drive Valerie and me and the control room nuts, but occasionally it was also the source of much laughter. One day after the show had been done live to the Maritimes, a problem with timing was discovered in the lead interview which meant that we would all have to stay in the studio and redo the whole hour for Quebec and Ontario. This sounds like typical television whining. And it is.

But director Sidney Cohen suggested a way out of the mess. If I simply went back on live to correct the timing of this particular question, we could all get out in another ten minutes. There was a lot of pressure being responsible for everyone's freedom, but all I had to do was repeat the question and take exactly 33 seconds doing it and I would be that day's lunch hero!

To tell you the truth, I don't remember the guest or the subject, although it might have been Keith Spicer and something to do with broadcast regulations. In any case, I remember only too clearly that part of the original question included the acronym "C.R.T.C."

As everyone held their breath, the moment of truth approached when we'd "break into" the tape feeding Ontario and Quebec, make the correction, and disappear.

I'll blame it on the adrenalin, because halfway through re-asking the question, I realized I had gone too fast and, watching the hand count of floor director Rene Dowhaniuk, I knew that I had to do something to make the question longer to fill in the 33 seconds.

The obvious change to make, inspired by such split-second terror, was to replace the shorthand version of the C.R.T.C., and to savor and linger on each word of that organization's title. I knew as soon as I said "Canadian Radio and ..." that I wasn't sure of the rest.

I still don't know what came out of my mouth, but it was something like the "Canadian Radio Commissh Telecommunicationvision and television coomunisyshtem kashon." Valerie had hung around for the drama and was still sitting beside me at the desk.

When she witnessed my tongue hitting the rhubarb and understanding well the unforgiving nature of the moment, she started to double over with laughter. It was all I could do not to crack up with her. It became even funnier when I realized that, of course, in real life, Spicer or whoever it was wouldn't have hesitated to correct my mangling of the title. But as he was already on tape, it was even more bizarre that he seemed oblivious to my stumbling.

In spite of my looking like a complete idiot, we achieved our goal and escaped the studio earlier than we might have that day. It certainly wasn't the only time I said the wrong thing.

One day, we had a champion breeder of Huskies on *Midday*. If I recall, her dogs had won the grueling Alaskan Iditarod race a number of times, and as we sat in the library set of *Midday*, one of her beautiful and well-behaved dogs lay at her feet.

About halfway through a five-minute conversation, I wanted to ask her about the genetic differences between male and female pups in terms of their predetermined ability to race. That's the question pretty much as I heard it in my mind, but it's not what came out of my mouth.

In the usual rush, rush, rush of television, I heard myself, unbelievably, asking in shorthand, "What's the difference between a male and female pup?"

Even though the control room was on the second level behind a cement block wall on the other side of this airplane hangar-sized studio, I heard director Sidney Cohen and colleagues explode in laughter.

I tried to disregard the commotion upstairs by listening and staring even more intently at the guest who politely "got" the question, but in spite of my concentration and out of the corner of my eye, I couldn't escape noticing that the floor director Rene Dowhaniuk was chuckling and writing something on a card.

I knew he would maneuver himself around the cameras, which incidentally now barely hid their bent-over and heaving operators. I also knew he was going to hold up the sign behind the guest, which meant, of course, I wouldn't be able to avoid seeing it as long as I was concentrating so intensely on this poor woman, who had no idea of the flurry of activity around her.

I can remember well that horrible feeling of trying not to laugh as I now saw Rene positioning himself behind the couch. Sure enough, he held up a piece of cardboard with the word "BALLS" on it, scribbled in big black letters. I was as relieved as a dog at the end of the Iditarod when that conversation ended.

I also began to notice that it wasn't only hosts who spoke differently on television. I would quite regularly go over to the radio building to see Gzowski and my friend Gary Katz early in the morning as they prepared for *Morningside*. In the constant buffet offered through promotional tours, it turned out we'd often be "doing" the same person on the same day.

I was always struck, if I managed to hear their conversation later that night on *The Best of Morningside*, by the difference in the tone of the encounter. It made me realize in a very practical way that even without a word being spoken, the camera had already changed the very nature of the exchange.

I don't know why that is, particularly. I just know it's true that someone with little to say could bomb on radio, but sparkle on television. And those with lots to say could shrink in front of the camera and blossom before a microphone. I suppose it all has to do with revealing insecurities and the power of the image over the word, but it never failed to surprise me.

As a result, the conversations on television never quite seemed as *real* for me as they did on radio. I remember a dear radio friend of mine asking me once, as we enjoyed the glorious sunshine on a Prince Edward Island beach, how it could be that I wasn't intimidated by the people I was then meeting.

I remember thinking, "But it's only television. We're not *really* meeting. It's more like we're actors putting on a show together." Anyway, I *do* think it takes extraordinary self-confidence to embrace television with any enthusiasm.

This eventually led me to the conclusion that the people who *weren't* nervous or insecure in front of a television camera were the people to approach with doubt.

Someone who could cut through all those elements with a sharp-edged verbal machete was the person whose dressing room was beside mine. I don't know that I've ever met anyone with a better *feel* for a story than the late Barbara Frum. When she wasn't busy, she was always welcoming if I stopped by for a chat in her dressing room.

I only worked with her a couple of times on *The Journal* and, like the audience, left admiring not only the obvious great skill with which she posed questions and demanded answers, but even more so, the sense of absolute control she brought to the situation.

If you, as a guest, thought for a split second you could get away with something, Frum was in your face immediately to advise you otherwise, and in no uncertain terms.

It was an education just listening to her handle people. If I recall correctly, it was former hippie and Chicago Seven defendant Jerry Rubin, now a Wall Street investment type, who tried to dismiss *her* motives as commercial and crass in a "whatever happened to the '60s?" kind of conversation.

She slam-dunked him without so much as a second's notice by responding icily, "And that's why you're doing this interview, is it, Mr. Rubin?"

Barbara Frum was an important figure in the broadcast life of this country but perhaps she meant even more to those of us *inside* the corporation. She had come to symbolize the very best of public broadcasting and I don't think it's an accident that the little weenies holding the purse and programming strings, within and without the corporation, suddenly became braver when she was gone.

Like Max and Allen were for me years before, Barbara Frum became a splendid role model who kept, front and centre, the concepts of integrity and fairness in a profession which rarely did itself proud.

But following her in interviews demonstrated just how differently we approached the work and how far apart were the roles we had adopted to play. I don't believe one approach is more *valid* than the other, but it was clear that *The Journal*'s "take no prisoners" philosophy was *valued* more as prime time material.

It was not unusual in those days for *The Journal* and *Midday* to coordinate resources and to do two *very* different interviews with the same person. (As I re-read that sentence, I have to smile and confess to a slight inaccuracy. We kind of piggybacked with *The Journal* when they said it was okay for us to do so.) Once with Rene Levesque and then later with the singer

Paul Simon, I wish I could have gone first. By the time I got to them, they had already gone 12 rounds with the reigning champion.

Just as working as a radio producer with Gzowski had taught me a great deal, this "piggy-backing" with *The Journal* allowed me to see, up close, Frum's techniques of preparation and interviewing. I recognized pretty quickly that her approach was not one I'd ever be comfortable using myself, but I knew enough by then that it was just as valuable to be aware of my limitations as my strengths.

Once or twice, I got to *be* Barbara on *The Journal*, as opposed to what was internally and accurately referred to as the "human cut-away" role. In the process, I learned how critical the packaging was to the final product and just how skilled *The Journal* producers were at creating an atmosphere of compelling immediacy and tension each night. Believe me, one day when I was Barbara, it felt like a dog's breakfast and yet that evening, *The Journal* would grab and hold your attention. The executive producer, Mark Starowicz, was as brilliant at creating a sense of urgency on *The Journal* as he had been years before on radio's *As It Happens*.

Interviews would be taped from about noon on, leaving *The Journal* producers the early evening to pick and choose the best and most provocative mix of material for that night's program. I remember one afternoon interviewing a ham radio operator, north of Toronto, who was in contact with some people attempting an Arctic adventure of some kind. As instructed by the hovering producer, I asked the guest what route these explorers would be following. I received an answer, but was told to ask the question again. I got another answer.

"Please ask it again and have him go through the route in detail," came word through my headset from the control room.

Imagine making love in a hotel at the same time the maid comes in to change the sheets, and you have a rough idea what this process is like.

"Just ask him again to tell us the route," the producer whispers again, this time a little tension creeping into her voice.

The poor fellow sitting north of Toronto can't see me nor can I see him, so there's no way to transfer the growing frustration on my part and no way to reassure him with body language that this is simply silly television stuff. All he hears, between the stretches of silence as the producer and I speak, is essentially the same question asked three times. The mystery is solved when the producer explains to me that the graphic, illustrating this northern journey, has already been done and doesn't correspond with what the guest is saying. At this late hour, it is easier to change the answer than the graphic. So I ended up telling the *guest* what his answer had to be!

I don't want to exaggerate the importance of this or leave the impression we were asking the guest to lie about the route. The producer felt the answer should precisely follow the graphic, with the hamlets and highlights of the Arctic area all mentioned in the exact same order. In the long run, this was yet one more experience with television's manipulation which only made me more uncomfortable doing it, not to mention more suspicious of almost everything anybody else did on it.

Even including, sometimes, the great ones like Barbara Frum. But those moments were rare. Frum's great gift, I think, was to bring a respect for and an integrity to the value of information. I don't recall ever seeing her own emotions cloud a story. In the same way that Walter Cronkite of CBS News distinguished himself when announcing John Kennedy's death or the moon landing by controlling his emotions, Frum never seemed to get caught in sentimentality or cheap emotionalism.

One of the qualities which seems to me, as a viewer, to be increasingly running television newsrooms these days, is a desperate desire to one-up the competition. A modern television news department virtually *creates* the news through the powerful resources at its fingertips, and then sells it is as being important.

Instead of going out and gathering the news of that day in the community and presenting the details fairly and accurately, television is increasingly involving *itself* in the process, which leaves us to watch the product of editorial meetings more than the actual news. There are times when I can't escape the conclusion that the anchor thinks his or her reaction to the story is as important as the event itself.

Sometimes, when everything is equal, silly things are tolerable. But when the equation of life shifts, the silly can become annoying, and I'm afraid that's what happened to my view of television. My sister was sick again, and my energies and interests were going in a different direction from those which occupied my working hours.

The small moments – a glance exchanged in a hospital hallway, a smile between worried friends at the end of the bed, the strangely intense comfort from the simple act of just being with someone – began to overwhelm me.

Although everyone at *Midday* couldn't have been more understanding, they and my job were getting in the way of where I wanted to be. The resentment began to build within me as I was kept from the real work I felt was calling me then.

The new world I entered that fall of 1987 could not have been further from the one I left. I had been leading such a privileged life, having, on a daily basis, the chance to speak with interesting and involved people across the country and working at a job where so much of the really hard work was already done by the time I sat, prepared by others, before the camera.

I honor my sister's memory and her privacy too much to go into any great detail about *her* world that fall, but I'm confident that all of you who've also lost a loved one to cancer know well the uncertain and painful journey it forces one to embark upon.

Even though I write these words almost ten years after she left us, the only thing I'm sure of is that my journey, which began with her death, is nowhere near the end. It was born of a sudden and acute awareness of life's fragility. I felt both frightened and awed before this new awareness, and kind of psychologically naked.

I guess, in moments of trauma, we all make promises to ourselves, keeping some and letting others slide away as the pain of the moment leaks from the heart. In the simplest way, mine was a dedication, essentially, to the opposite of the experience I had been through. I vowed to devote myself in her memory to behavior and ideas which had *creation*, not destruction, at their root.

My "job" seemed to me to be all about ego, period. But at the same time, the "work" of finding my path through the challenging mysteries of the universe, now the feature attraction showing on the screen of my consciousness, was making the importance of ego so laughably small and utterly insignificant that I struggled to take any of it seriously.

After so many years of having my ego fed by such a public job and finally seeing it for what it was, I desperately needed to find something which at least *felt* like it might have a little more substance to it than television. Having to show up at *Midday* to be part of this "happy couple" only continued to increase my anger and frustration.

I took much of this personal storm out on Valerie and I regret that. No one can sustain forever the intensity experienced in losing a loved one and sometimes the decisions made during such stress aren't the right ones. But sometimes they are. Leaving *Midday* was what I had to do.

I don't want to leave the impression I left the program only because my sister died. That's unfair to her memory. But clearly, a switch had been flipped within me, illuminating a new path, signalling a new direction.

There are infrequent moments when I wish I had been able to get through these changes in my life without sacrificing so much, but that's not how it happened. My faith that, in the end, everything happens for a reason, is as deep as my regret over the way I left my friends at *Midday*.

I had no idea what I was going to do, and never in my wildest imagination did I think it would be another television program.

But then I heard that Roy Bonisteel was leaving *Man Alive*.

NINE

"MAN ... WHAT?"

To a remarkable extent, television people and programs exist on nothing but perception. This giant electronic mirage shimmers in the desert of popular culture, its bluish glow attracting humans the way a fire pulls in lions in the Kalahari.

As the embers of that desert fire die and the eyes adapt to the deepening darkness, the form of the lions takes shape. But the constant hypnotic glow from the mirage of television never dies, never allowing sight beyond its promise.

And the promise of *Man Alive* was very enticing. Although I don't think I had ever actually watched an episode from start to finish, I shared with so many other Canadians the view that it was a well-intentioned program that dealt with serious questions in a sensitive and, dare I say it, intelligent way.

I think to some extent the very fact that it existed, like Canada's north or Stephen Hawking's *Brief History of Time*, was enough. We didn't have to go there or read it or watch it to be reassured by its cosmic presence.

I had met and liked Roy Bonisteel. He seemed honest and straightforward and mercifully unburdened by his celebrity. In addition, over the years Roy had developed on television that rare, priceless, and sought-after quality of credibility.

"Priceless," because in the theatrics of television, one character must be the truth teller. It's not something that can be taught or ordered.

"Okay. We're coming to you in five, four, three – remember, look credible – two, one ..."

The concept of credibility is one I remember having fun discussing with the American media critic and educational observer Neil Postman. As we sat in his New York office, he wondered what we actually mean when we say, for example, that a news anchor on television lacks credibility.

"Do we feel the anchor doesn't *believe* what they're reading?" Postman asked. "Or is it that they don't *understand* the actual content of the news?"

I asked a friend, also working in television at the time, how she gauged credibility. I think I heard the perfect television response when she answered that credibility is how the poor soul left on camera reacts if the TelePrompTer lifeline suddenly breaks.

I'm assuming the TelePrompTer is no longer a secret to viewers, but in case it is to you, allow me a very quick description. Ninety-nine point nine nine nine per cent of what you hear on television has been scripted and is scrolled back in a little window, situated under the lens of the camera through which the coifed head of the moment talks to you.

Which means that much of the skill of a television host watching these words roll by is to look as if they're not actually watching these words roll by, even though everybody *knows* that's what they're doing. Reading.

You've all seen that happen, when the person on camera is left looking like a terrified deer caught in the glaring highbeam headlights of an on-rushing Mack truck. When that umbilical chord between the TelePrompTer and the host is cut, the previously safe "womb" in the warmth and comfort of a television studio, becomes a space as uninviting as a prison with progressively shrinking walls.

Even though it has happened to me and its memory still brings beads of sweat to my brow, it remains one of my favorite and one of the most revealing moments of television because, at that precise moment, the jig is exposed. Reality enters, with all the freshness of a summer breeze off the Atlantic. Suddenly, the painstakingly-built television house of cards collapses and the anchor is transformed from the articulate, confident, and knowledgeable smoothie to Marcel Marceau, a painted face with no words.

There are so many elements in a television production, even in the studio, which can so easily go wrong, it's fairly critical for "the face" to be able to lend the "make-believe" proceedings a degree of believability or credibility.

Multiply that requirement for a program like *Man Alive*, forced not only to deal with the vagaries of working in the field, but also engaged with subject matter often of a sensitive and personal nature. That perception of integrity is what Roy Bonisteel brought to the screen in spades.

Many of my experiences following Roy as host of *Man Alive* were so intense, it's difficult for me now to think of the time when I knew nothing about it or the people behind its production. But this much is clear.

The journey began when, regrettably, I made two assumptions which then seemed quite valid and reasonable. Still do, when I think about it. I try not to think about it. First, if the program was looking for a host, which it was, then it seemed to follow that it actually *wanted* one. Second, if the program was talking to *me* about the job, which it was, it wanted a working host/journalist. It was certainly the view I had of Roy's role and contribution.

What I learned in the weeks to come was that they really would have preferred only a figurehead, someone to take their work and deliver it to the audience without frightening old people or young children. My God, I'd become the Governor-General!

So I certainly had no inside or even hard information about the workings of *Man Alive*. Only the belief that it dealt in the subject matter which now held more promise for me than yelling at finance ministers. I am someone who doesn't *become* "a journalist" when I go through the doors to work. I bring with me and use, as a kind of barometer, my own life experience, and like you, I'm sure, the questions which matter change as the pages of life are turned. I thought I was on the same page as *Man Alive*.

Within CBC television, *Man Alive* enjoyed the kind of Teflon coating that CBC radio and certain prime ministers and presidents have taken advantage of in recent years. Part of that protective coating comes from the fact that nobody wants to be seen to be attacking a show that purports to celebrate the human spirit. It would be too much like swarming *Mister Rogers' Neighborhood*.

Two other factors worked in *Man Alive*'s favor. It was a relatively cheap program to produce and it helped fulfill the mandate of the CBC's license to broadcast, in that it could claim to be representing all parts of the Canadian community. It allowed those from the corporation who had to appear before various interest groups such as the religious advisory panel to point to *Man Alive* as an example of its commitment to religious programming. For a number of reasons, the program enjoyed a relatively safe existence and got an almost free ride from most everyone. Yet in response to the pressures of shrinking budgets and implicit demands for larger audience numbers, the program began to concentrate on the sensationalism of victims, and not on the inspiration of survivors. My name became attached to material which embarrassed me.

Following her dire warnings about the characters on staff, though, I half expected to walk into the bar scene from *Star Wars* when senior producer Louise Lore called our first meeting together. While the producers were understandably concerned about a new host and what that might mean for their "highly personal style of work" – Lore's words, not mine – I thought from the very beginning that we'd be able to work out some kind of acceptable relationship. And although it took four years, I think, in the end, we managed to do just that.

When a show has been on the air for as long as *Man Alive* has been, it takes a deliberate effort and commitment to move it into new territory. That effort and commitment can only flow from leadership which embraces the challenges of change and recognizes how vital it is to keep fresh air and ideas bubbling up through the system.

Failing that will to move forward and to remain apart from much of the television schedule by concentrating on *Man Alive*'s unique mandate, I'm afraid the show became a bit lazy and began to rely on clichés. If the program had ever been adventurous and daring, and actually *Alive* as I had thought, those days seemed long gone by the time I arrived on the scene.

My ego was large enough, though, that I thought I could change it and that I would eventually be able to drag *Man Alive*, even if it was kicking and screaming, to stake out its new territory. Needless to say, I underestimated the forces defending the status quo.

The program had become so completely a forum for personal expression that the idea we had an obligation to the audience – which paid us – was utterly inconsequential, and seen as a somewhat quaint notion.

Little could I possibly have realized that this period would seem inspired compared to what followed. If you want a practical example of what's happened to CBC television, you need look no further for clues than the introduction of R.H. Thompson as the current host of *Man Alive*.

Please don't misunderstand. This has nothing to do with R.H. Thompson. I think he's a splendidly gifted actor, if not the country's best. That's not the question. The problem is precisely that he *is* one of Canada's best actors. His essential talent is deception, manufacturing emotion and making you believe it's genuine. The show that explored and celebrated *belief* now asks you, with a straight face, to suspend that belief and watch an acting job.

It would not surprise me and it would be almost deserved if, by the time you read these words, the program is no longer on the television schedule. I say "almost" because the potential of that show is still close to my heart, and I think its idea is needed now more than ever before.

It will certainly not be Thompson's fault if one of Canada's most respected and longest running television efforts disappears. That honor will rest squarely on the shoulders of management.

Man Alive once stood out precisely because it wasn't television as usual. It not only tolerated but encouraged, it seemed to me, those awkward and non-television moments which reveal the strength and folly of human nature.

What a long and sad journey it is to have reached a point where the primary reason for having a particular person tell you a story is his ability to make *you* believe that *he* actually believes what he's saying. If it catches on, I can't wait for "*The National* – with Christopher Plummer.*"

Even more than trivializing the audience, this kind of mentality on a once-respected program like *Man Alive* treats real and vulnerable people, struggling with profoundly difficult life choices and situations, as nothing more than emotional cattle on the way to the big television abattoir in the sky, with its endless appetite for spilled guts and feelings.

The essence of tackling life's big questions, it increasingly seems to me, is a process of removing our masks. This kind of television-as-theater is all about adding layers of deceit, layering one more mask upon another.

I'm willing to listen to the argument that I may have expected too much from it and took it too seriously, but you know, that desire only comes from the experience I had that television can deliver the goods when it's in the proper hands.

This much time after the fact, my mind skims over some of the *Man Alive* stories like a flat stone on a mirrored lake, but certain people and events still invite me to wade in deeper pools of reflection and understanding.

There weren't really many of those "eureka" moments of sudden revelation for me, although I do remember once in Haiti, when we got caught screaming down a mountain with strangers in a broken down Chevy, trying to beat the curfew one night. The simple revelation that came to me at that moment, as a hub cap flew off the taxi on a tight corner, was that we were going to go flying off the cliff or get shot by the army. Either way, I'd be getting the last make-up job any second now.

Aside from that experience, the continuing impact of having worked on *Man Alive* has been as subtle as the ocean tides, still nudging my life slowly and almost invisibly in a new direction – a direction which, ironically, would have me leaving the very work which set me on its path in the first place. Juggling that kind of good and bad consequence pretty well reflects my feelings these days about the media generally and television specifically.

The demands to get going on the 1989 season of programs outweighed any personal worries raised during my first few months. A television documentary show is to a studio show what licorice is to a porcupine. They have such completely different demands and requirements, I was stunned during those first weeks by the questions neither Lore nor I had bothered to ask each other.

My saving grace that spring was the presence of producer Robin Taylor, who had been, for so many years, the spine and the conscience of the much celebrated and honored current affairs program *The Fifth Estate*. I used to bump into him around the *Midday* studios, but we'd never met or spoken until he too joined *Man Alive*.

Of Robin's many qualities, his integrity is what impressed me the most. He has a mind that leaps on an idea like a rested cat on a tired mouse and he is absolutely relentless in his demand and expectation that logic and reason prevail in every argument. This quality guaranteed that he would disagree volubly with the more intuitive types at *Man Alive* who believed "journalism" was a four-letter word.

This sometimes entertaining collision between logic and emotion reached its peak in one of our meetings, following the broadcast of a program where various people, who claimed to have been abducted by aliens – always a ratings winner – came together in a neutral location and "amazingly" described similar-looking beings from the spaceship.

I confess that I shared with the producer of this piece the wonder at the similarities of these abduction stories. Robin's valuable, blunt response, following the oohing and ahhing (mine included) over how people who had never met and who lived thousands of miles apart could come together to describe the same alien face, was to blurt out, "But for God's sake, haven't you heard of the _ _ _ _ telephone?"

It was a tough but entertaining "family," on days like this.

Robin's enthusiasm for committing the act of journalism and his conviction that public broadcasting carried with it serious responsibilities was contagious. His belief that it was more important to find out what someone was going to *do* about a situation rather than how they *felt* about it was clearly introducing a new edge to the program, one which had the old hands a tad nervous. It was a journalistic approach closer to my experience, if not my heart, and so I felt quite comfortable with him.

He and I set out on our first *Man Alive* assignment together to Newfoundland, where the communities, more than the Catholic Church, were reeling from stories of priests sexually abusing young boys. Little did I know then that I would hear echoes from the issues and situations raised in this first story again and again during my years at the program.

Among these recurring themes, in a very general way for now, were the comfort and strength which people found in community, how it takes courage to hold on to one's *convictions* in a world of compromise, the critical role that *hope* plays in human existence, and the power of a *personal* faith.

The institution of the church and all it promised and stood for was once at the very centre of life in the many small communities in Newfoundland. As we sat in the kitchen of one house in Portugal Cove, the imposing, and I suppose once-comforting, view of the church on the hill was inescapable through the window over the sink.

Aware of the abuse the young man of the house had endured at the hands of the priest from that church, the building now appeared to crouch ominously over the community, no longer symbolizing the glory of God, but the deprivation of "man."

The parents of the abused boy remembered how the priest would sometimes call late at night to ask if their son might come up the hill to help him out. The father held back tears when he said he never gave the request a second thought, certain that it was better for his son to be involved with the church than hanging around street corners. Consequently, he would always allow the boy to go.

The mother of this young man stared out the window at the church on the hill and finally said, quietly, but with fierce determination, that she would never, never, *ever* set foot in that building again. But more importantly, she added that nothing had damaged her faith or shaken her belief in God.

At the time, I confess, I thought privately, "But how could you possibly still believe in a merciful God when your son has had this happen to him?" Even as I became more confident with this subject matter in these kinds of conversations and would sometimes ask that question or a variation of it out loud, I came to learn that there's no satisfactory explanation of why suffering exists in this world.

And I'm not sure I'm entirely satisfied with the concept of allowing it to remain one of life's mysteries, that it's something we're not meant to understand. There is so much needless pain and suffering around the world that it remains a source of great anger for me. I never understood that the child who lies down at night with hunger and sorrow anywhere in the world wasn't my child. Maybe *Man Alive* was a way for me not to feel helpless, a way for me to work through such corrosive emotions.

While I was moved by the tears in the eyes of proud people and angered by the arrogance and indifference of men hiding behind their collars, it was a new idea to me that people could separate their faith from their church.

In my simplicity in these matters, it seemed to me then that you couldn't ignore the grocery store while needing its food. The people of Newfoundland, in a very early lesson, taught me to make the distinction.

Like the hardware of television, the bureaucracy of faith, I learned, takes advantage of its power and attraction, but contributes almost nothing to the nature of the experience. The church has as little to do with God as the grocery store has with nourishment.

In a personal way, I had already begun to examine my own beliefs and ideas about what it meant to live a life of some worth and consequence. Professionally, this first trip with *Man Alive* to Newfoundland added that new wrinkle.

I don't have all the answers yet, but I think for that inner part of our lives to be genuine, it must come from within first. Our spiritual life is like a tiny bulb buried under seven feet of snow. We have, within us already, all the elements necessary for it to blossom, but it won't if we fool ourselves with easy substitutions. Like the bulb, our own "blossoming" requires time and the right ingredients to appear in all its beauty.

That personal centre has to be felt even through the excess of life, because it may only brush your heart with the softest touch, or reach your ear through all the noise of this world with the gentlest of whispers.

I saw how the force and immediacy of one's faith develops in direct relation to the proximity of the external threat against it. It was as true in the windswept houses and souls of Newfoundland as it was in an old stone church in the small town of Timisoara in Romania.

As if cutting the cancer from a sick body, the Romanian people rid themselves of their despised dictators, the Ceausescus, by firing squad on Christmas Day 1989, ending the Ceausescus' 25-year reign of terror.

We read reports of a Reformed Hungarian Protestant minister named Laszlo Tokes and of how his outspoken criticism of government policy had made him a marked man in a society which marked citizens all too easily.

His public declarations had resulted in an order from the authorities, both church and state, to leave his parish and to essentially disappear in the remote Romanian countryside.

We read, too, that he had been supported mainly by his parishioners, but by other people as well, who locked arms and surrounded his small church to protect him in the face of a cruel and brutal tyranny. His unwavering faith and those it inspired made others brave enough to ignite the revolution.

In January of 1990, we flew to Budapest, picked up a van and then drove a few hours back to the fifth century. That's only a slight exaggeration. We headed toward Timisoara, the small western Romanian town with little place in history until Tokes and his friends started the impossible. It was now known around the world as the birthplace of the revolution.

It is not easy to describe the assault on the human spirit we witnessed in that nation. Arriving late at night in a place where even the little electric power available was rationed, we crawled along the darkened streets as the shapes of people would suddenly jump out of the darkness at us, like in a carnival ride, and then just as quickly disappear again in the shadows.

It was a place that breathed paranoia, where friends wouldn't dare to speak to each other even on the street, worried that some informer might report the exchange. Only the ever-present prostitutes in the hotel looked happy.

The offical church here, as in Newfoundland, had not acted in a noble and determined way on the side of its believers. The level of collusion between its hierarchy and Ceausescu's thugs, to this day, remains a disgrace.

It was the *institution* of religion which had failed again, and in spite of the far different circumstances in completely separate worlds, betrayal is still betrayal. And so the story of Laszlo Tokes and the survival of his "personal" faith, in a mostly discredited institution, seemed all the more remarkable to me. It had inspired his congregation to risk their lives to protect his.

When the citizens of Timisoara had been abused to the point where death was preferable to the existence they endured, they stood and faced the army's bullets in *Libertate*, or "Freedom Square." I recall hearing from an eyewitness how frightening it was to watch these people *not* run, but simply stand before the army, defiantly chanting "Down with Ceausescu" and "Freedom."

By the time we arrived in the square, the steps of the church at one end of the gathering place were virtually made of wax. But the thousands of melted candles lit to commemorate the dead still couldn't cover the shame of what had happened there.

I walked quietly through the sorrow and the grief and wondered about my responsibility. The more detached, professional part of me knew a good story when it saw one. And this was a good story. The other more troublesome part of my conscience wanted to respect the privacy of such tragedy.

People were silently clutching photographs or candles or flowers, and their tear-stained, troubled faces revealed a pain and a hardship I'd never seen before.

The producer and I stood there exchanging only a few words, but apparently enough to attract the attention of a young woman named Mihila. She asked if she might practice her English with us by helping with translations and so on.

Our relationship with her resulted in an invitation to spend an evening with her husband and mother and father in the apartment they all shared together. We would learn later that we were the first Westerners they had allowed themselves to meet, braver now following the Christmas executions.

Remarkably, the fact that her parents spoke no English didn't seem to have any effect on the conversation. We all sat in this tiny room around a table where they so generously shared what little food was available. It is a night I'll never forget, where not even words, and certainly no television cameras, were needed to share our lives.

Their spirit, which had somehow survived the long years of brutal starvation, left all of us – certainly me – with a fresh appreciation for its mysterious power, and it provided a new perspective on my own quality of life.

I stood in Tokes' Hungarian Reformed Church in Timisoara for his first sermon following the revolution, shoulder to shoulder with the brave souls devoted to him and to the cause of justice.

Some had undergone months of interrogation and harassment from the brutal secret police. Others who couldn't get in the packed church that chilly morning, but who wanted to touch and feel this new freedom, stood silently in the street, grasping the tiny paper notice of the sermon like a cherished photograph, worried that if they let go, this unbelievable dream might end.

On this same tree-lined street not so very long before, the tanks had gathered and tear gas had been released to terrorize these parishioners into staying at home. But even that hadn't worked against the gloriously stubborn power of their faith.

It was a moment like this when all the fancy words of the academics and all the intricate arguments of brilliant philosophers around the world against the power of faith and belief in God, became, for me at least, meaningless in the face of experience.

I walked along the street and stopped beside an elderly woman who stood motionless, listening to the voice of Reverend Tokes on the bad speakers set up by the front doors of the church. She had wrapped a scarf around her head to protect her face against the cold, so only her eyes showed. They were red with exhaustion, and giant tears streamed down her cheeks.

For so many reasons, the psalm Tokes read that morning

had a special meaning for this woman and for all the others who had endured such hardship under the Ceausescus.

The pastor said, in his almost shy way, "With the Lord on my side, I do not fear. What can man do to me?"

All Romanians, but especially the Hungarian minority within the country, knew only too well the horrible answer.

Tokes was born in a town now called Cluj-Napoca, the old and once spirited Hungarian capital of Transylvania, in the northern area of Romania. Nicolae Ceausescu had been determined to break that spirit by closing Hungarian schools, universities, and newspapers in what he planned as a forced assimilation. He wanted nothing short of a repressed and defeated population.

We wanted to leave Timisoara to visit Tokes' mother and father, himself a minister and professor of theology. The pastoral beauty we passed on the way north hid the almost medieval cruelty of modern Romanian life.

We soon found ourselves in the thickest fog imaginable, inching our way along winding mountain roads in the dead of night. There was plenty of time, after my elegantly subdued birthday party in the van, to sit and reflect on what we had seen so far.

My mind was still on something which had happened that afternoon. We had had lunch with Mihila and her husband at our hotel, one which they had previously not been allowed to enter. I think they were a bit surprised but satisfied when they realized they hadn't been missing much.

We had agreed to pay them a tiny bit of money for helping us out and so as we walked out after lunch with Mihila still nervous about public actions, she suggested we sit in the van for the transaction. I was completely unprepared for her reaction when I handed her an American $20 bill.

She became very emotional and said she had only dreamed that one day she'd hold a bill of American currency. It suddenly hit me just how completely isolated her life had been from the rest of the world.

Now, it's always possible that she would go through the same routine with another television crew later that afternoon, but I don't think so. She seemed so genuinely grateful and touched that I believed her and learned a great deal from our short friendship.

It's funny how the mind responds when exposed to stories of cruelty and deprivation. Our first morning in Cluj-Napoca, the cameraman grabbed me and said with great excitement that he had seen *them* burying bodies at the side of the hotel. We went to have a closer look and had to pretend to be interested as the new *trees* arrived to be planted in the waiting holes.

Tokes' family welcomed us warmly and his father, especially, was impressed by what he called his son's "obedience" – not to himself, he quickly added, but to his Lord. He said that was what was at the centre of his son's extraordinary courage.

Again, the business of television created a ridiculous situation with this man, already under such great pressure. We had to move the camera around so I could re-ask the questions and I think we told Father Tokes a hundred times that he didn't have to answer the questions again. All he had to do was listen.

We never were able to explain the procedure to him and he must have thought I was completely crazy continuing to ask questions, but then not wanting his answers. I ended that day with a hole – okay, maybe a dent – in my chest from where, in his frustration, Father Tokes had repeatedly poked me with his finger.

The idea that the television camera, by its very presence, changes the dynamics of any situation hardly needs to be repeated. But I'll tell you it is quite astonishing to see that actually happen for the first time, as I did in Romania that winter.

A crowd of largely disinterested young men would be standing around smoking and laughing at a political rally of one stripe or another. As soon as the camera appeared, they would transform themselves into political animals, shouting and screaming their anger or support – who could tell which? – and acting with real conviction.

And then, just as quickly, when the camera was put away, they'd resume their "at ease" stance and simply be a bunch of kids in the square. It made me terribly uncomfortable and suspicious of almost everything I see happen on television.

Again, just last night, I watched a CBS reporter from the new Democratic Republic of Congo, formerly Zaire, say that they had chosen to turn the camera off that afternoon. It seemed that the roving and vengeful crowds, searching for former Mobutu operatives, were only too willing to inflict a beating on someone – anyone – for the reporter's sake. I bet she doesn't last long with that kind of crazy attitude.

I witnessed and worried about that astonishing power of the television camera, again and again, at home and around the world. It is no longer simply a "recorder" of events. It has become *the* way to state your case on the world's stage.

One of the conversations from Romania which has stayed with me took place in a dark room with a dark man. He was a friend of and advisor to Tokes and, as such, still had to be very careful with his words and thoughts, as no one could be entirely sure where Ceausescu's cockroaches had scurried for cover.

As if it were yesterday, I recall sitting across the desk and understanding for perhaps the first time in a real way just how desperately, achingly hard that life had been for him. I listened to his anger and felt the courage of his words.

"It is easy to speak of democracy and justice in front of television in the West," he said softly, but not accusingly. "It is not so easy to fight the Securitate on the streets of Romania."

It was a very moving lesson about having the courage to stand up against such corruption and evil. This man risked his life taking information from Tokes, who was then imprisoned in his church, to Hungary so the world would know what was happening in Timisoara.

Sitting with him, I realized that we were about the same age, but our lives couldn't have been more different. And I wondered if crisis reveals or builds faith. Was I willing to die for something? Anything? How could I make my comfortable life mean something, stand for something? My silent questions ended when he almost smiled about the future of Romania, but said, "You know, you can't build a democracy based on lies."

I understood then, as that mother had so clearly done in Portugal Cove, that *real* faith must rest in your heart, on a personal, unshakable truth, one which has nothing to do with the structure or authority of any institution.

The damage done by the church in Newfoundland oozed across the island like an oil spill. Clearly, families had been damaged, the larger community was bruised and aching, but in spite of all the hurt, the church did nothing to alleviate any of the pain and suffering its agents had caused.

The dithering archbishop in St. John's was no longer speaking publicly and had assigned a smooth talker to deal with the dreaded media. I recall walking with this priest around the side of his church on that hill in Portugal Cove and, having turned the corner, hearing him say, "It's okay, we're out of the shot now."

This is a man who has clearly been taken by the celebrity conferred upon him by television, I thought to myself. It is such an easy and corruptible path to follow that by the time any awareness sinks in, priorities have already been turned upside down – and all of it done to accommodate that bloody camera.

We finished our work in Newfoundland and returned to Toronto with a number of stories from families, therapists, and the church. But we discovered a problem with the opening.

Our openings to the show were generally about 30 seconds long, usually done in some picturesque setting that would establish the place of the story. We had done the opening to Robin's and my first *Man Alive* program outside the impressive and imposing basilica in downtown St. John's. The size of it alone seemed to establish the weight and presence of the church on the island, so we were quite happy with the choice.

It turned out to be one of those afternoons with the sudden and amazingly strong gusts of wind common to the east coast which could sneak up and almost knock you over. No longer pampered by the presence of a hairdresser, this situation called for an extra heavy-duty dose of hair spray, I told myself, not having a clue. I ended up on the street by the basilica wearing a helmet as much as hair.

This meant that not one hair would or could move by itself. Unfortunately, we only saw once we got back to the editing suite in Toronto that every time I got hit by a gust of wind and my hair moved as one, it looked like I had an old arthritic muskrat trying to find a comfortable spot on my head.

So we were faced with trying to find a location around Toronto which could pass for a spot in Newfoundland. They do it all the time in movies, of course, and I thought that as long as we were careful not to say during the opening anything like "here in Newfoundland," it was okay to create the impression we wanted to create.

We located an old church in the Forest Hills area of Toronto and were about to set up when Robin suggested we inform someone inside of our plans. The person who went in to check that it was alright for us to shoot the wall of the church, without identifying it, came out and announced the church wanted $200 to "loan" us the ten square feet of wall we needed.

Clearly, it is not only angry mobs in Africa whose behavior is changed by the television camera. Like the taxi driver in Tuktoyaktuk when I was with *Midday*, they saw us coming, but this time we didn't pay. Robin and I shared an impatience with the process of television so we both quickly decided to do the opening in a nearby park. They have trees in Newfoundland, right? Their blossoming would be about the same, right? Good. Let's go and get this _ _ _ _ thing done.

What we hadn't counted on was the choir of curious bird voices our arrival elicited in the park. We stood there worrying that a certain species of bird, never before located in Newfoundland, would suddenly sing its song in the background of our little opening, sending attentive ornithologists into frenzied but unwarranted excitement.

It was situations and conversations like this one which would have me dreading the question "What did you do at the office today?"

There were producers for whom this would have been a major, hand-wringing event but again, bless Robin, we got through it with the shout of only one pushy blue jay in the background. It was to be the first of many interesting experiences – often involving the opening sequence and caused by a television camera – that Robin and I would have together.

On another occasion, we traveled to India together to do a story about Fred and Bonnie Cappucino's Child Haven organization, which operates homes for destitute women and children. Near the end of our time at their home in Hyderabad, we chose one of the busiest streets in that city of around five million people and ten million water buffalo for the opening.

We knew when we returned to Canada we'd be visiting Fred and Bonnie at their farm in Maxville, Ontario, and thought the quiet of their home would contrast nicely with the enormous racket on this street.

As it turned out, the diesel fumes got to Robin and he went back to sit in the car to try to lose his headache. I was left with our Indian crew standing on this impossibly narrow curb in the middle of this tumult and shouting the opening to the program.

Maybe if Robin had been there we would have done it again, because when we returned to the silence of the editing suite at 790 Bay Street in Toronto, there was one version of the opening which featured, completely unbeknownst to me, a huge water buffalo slowly lumbering across the screen, just inches behind me.

The trouble is I stopped half way through this version to correct something. By the time I did it again properly, our mud-covered visitor had left. For some reason, Robin had developed a real affection for these huge beasts, which were everywhere around Hyderabad, and he tried every trick in the book to use the opening in which one had made an all too brief appearance.

I cherished the chances I had to work with Robin. He's one of the most entertaining people you'd ever hope to meet and so it wasn't unusual on our shoots that the day would end around a table with a few drinks and much laughter.

Once, in Lethbridge, Alberta, after a difficult day spent working on a story about teenage suicide and Satanism, we were all relaxing in the bar of our hotel.

We had seen an incredible sunset the night before and had decided that it should be the background to the opening of the story. The weather conditions seemed right for another lovely sunset but, as usual, one thing led to another.

When somebody finally noticed the time, we all raced out to the parking lot like the Marx Brothers, scrambled about like maniacs, and shot the opening with only seconds to spare before losing the heavenly background.

Once again, another notch on the old belt of deception. This opening looked remarkably calm and deliberate by the time it made it to your television.

The show from Newfoundland opened my first season of *Man Alive* and I was pleased that it sent a slightly different signal to the audience. Critics were universally kind about my taking over from Roy and seemed inclined to give me the benefit of the doubt, which is more than I could have asked for.

Despite a few bumps at the beginning, the promise of *Man Alive*, like the lions around the fading glow in the desert, was taking shape. As my eyes adjusted to the new light, I began to see more clearly the kinds of people and stories I wanted to investigate.

TEN

THE LANGUAGE OF FAITH

I found it interesting at first and then curious how even *mouthing* the word "religion" in almost any room, but certainly one full of television producers, carried the weight and alarm of shouting "fire" in a packed theater. With the possible exception of settling travel expenses or of hearing about the dreaded annual meeting, nothing else could empty a room faster at *Man Alive*.

Given the outlandish expression of religion on television specifically, and, more generally, the ridicule directed at expression of faith in North America, this, I suppose, can't qualify as a surprise.

As someone who hosted a prime time television program often devoted to matters of the human spirit, I feel equipped to testify, although he doesn't need it, on behalf of American academic Stephen Carter, who has written about the North American culture of disbelief.

There's simply no question that to the substantial extent our culture is nourished by television, the result in terms of a religious meal is profound indigestion. That's assuming it hasn't already completely starved those who may be hungry for something with a little more substance to it.

After all, religion on television, aside from the exaggerated clowns who will sell heaven this very second if you call 1-800-THE-LORD, only appears on newscasts.

"A poll released today shows fewer Canadians are attending a mainstream church than ... blah, blah, blah ..."

"No one in this small, loyal congregation could ever have suspected that their caring and loving Reverend Snake had, in fact, been leading a double life when it was discovered he ..."

This reluctance to say the word "religion" out loud at *Man Alive* resulted in a variety of euphemisms being used, and perhaps necessitates a word or two here about language. The word "spirituality" is used extensively these days and has been called, by some, the perfect plastic word for our consumer society.

One result of this overuse and abuse of the word "spirituality" is that it ends up meaning whatever the person who says it wants it to mean, and that can end up involving everything from New Age channeling to rejection of materialism to near-death experiences to traditional church services to alien abductions. Now *that's* a "spiritual" smorgasbord.

One of my first tasks on virtually every shoot with *Man Alive* was to try to discover what each particular guest meant when he or she used the "S" word. The more people felt like they had to distance themselves from any connection with the so-called official church, the more confusing it got.

Certainly, the Christian church is in a period of profound and difficult transformation, but, minus the religious baggage so many carry around, the questions we human beings all face and continue to struggle with haven't changed: "What does it really mean to be alive? How does one live with doubt? Is there a God? What happens when we die?"

In broad strokes, *Man Alive* was charged with uncovering the great variety of ways people had come to discover some meaning in their lives. In other words, how, in part, they answered those age-old questions. So while I wouldn't go as far as dismissing the word spirituality as "plastic" or meaningless, I wish there was another one to accurately describe this human desire.

Part of *Man Alive*'s wonderful legacy is that it helped me understand that the profound richness of a spiritual life comes, not from finding one truth and holding onto it for evermore, but from acknowledging many truths and respecting the paths others have chosen to follow.

Regardless of language, I started to learn to gauge my own spiritual maturity by my willingness to keep my heart open and receptive so I could hear the footsteps on the paths taken by others. This was more work than I anticipated, as it always is when we choose to *think* rather than only accept.

And *Man Alive* made me think about it. Even had I wanted to remain detached from the material, I don't think I could have managed it. By the time my first season ended, I needed time off just to try to rearrange the file cards in my head.

There were times I felt like the journalistic equivalent of Milli Vanilli. And the experience that first year *was* frustrating and overwhelming, but it was also largely fulfilling. It was not unlike being turned inside out, or at least how I imagine that must feel.

It's a shame that we often get so tangled up in the language surrounding religion, we miss the point of the conversation. It seemed to me that the point of *Man Alive*, even with all the limitations and restrictions imposed by television, was to communicate an aspect or dimension of spiritual life.

Maybe I didn't do such a good job in demanding that we clearly articulate what we were about. I think there were times we were not only linguistically lazy, but also philosophically lazy.

The truth is, given the rest of the television line-up, there wasn't much competition for the subject matter, so we could allow ourselves to slide occasionally. This hesitation and kind of stuttering around religious/spiritual issues taught me something. You can't have a substantial talk about something as important as these questions of meaning if you bury them under euphemisms and spend your energies dancing all around them.

So to avoid any confusion when I use the word spiritual, and at the risk of attack for baring my soul, here's what I mean. I believe there is a power, greater than all of us combined, at work in the universe. I think our lives have to mean something, that we're here on this planet at this time for a reason. I believe we are more than just a series of chemical reactions and electrical connections wrapped in epidermal layers waiting to rot in the ground.

I believe in wonder, and yes, even miracles. And while it still gives me trouble on sleepless nights, I've grudgingly come to accept the existence of mystery, that there are aspects of life which shall remain unexplained to me – and perhaps, even to a television producer.

I think the awareness of the sacred all around us can only be ours when we let go of everything, just as love sometimes arrives only when we stop looking for it. And finally, I believe that "The Answer," if it exists, is not out there with some guru on a mountaintop in India – as helpful as that might be – but it's already inside each of us. Our great work in life, it seems to me, is the process of discovering and letting it out.

When it comes to the more problematic question of faith, I like the answer given me by the Anglican minister and physicist John Polkinghorne, in a conversation I had with him in Montreal. I had asked this religious scientist a question about how faith involved a leap of some kind, a suspension of rational belief. He replied that it was at least a leap into the light. I can live with that.

There. Now I've let that out. Yes, the church has caused a great deal of trouble in this world, wars have been fought and lives lost in the name of belief. Yes, there are unscrupulous "religious" characters who prey on and take advantage of the vulnerable in our world. Yes, religion can be intolerant and arrogant and cruel. But all of that is about the *institution* of faith. I want the *experience*.

One of my wickedly favorite moments as host of the *Man Alive*, when of course it wasn't me trying to answer the question, was to watch the producers struggle to explain what the show was about without using the "R" word. The verbal gymnastics were truly something to behold.

Following the broadcast of any program, about which even the verbal equivalent of Nadia Comaneci couldn't have avoided using the word – or even a program which might have remotely praised or cut the church a little slack – I would get very angry mail accusing me of fuzzy thinking and of being a dupe of "organized religion," as it was always phrased. As if it were organized crime.

There's no question hundreds of thousands have been terribly damaged and psychically assaulted by their religious experience. I don't close my eyes or my mind to that reality. It just seems to me that the people who are no longer even willing to listen are just as wrong as those within the church community who believe they only have to find the right language to get the congregation back.

Man Alive served up an interesting contradiction. On the one hand, it was a very public exercise which gave me a higher profile than *Midday*, and the attention it brought me was pleasant, although embarrassing at times. I was a celebrity nerd – once illustrated on a long flight somewhere, when the attendant, who had recognized me, came back and said, "Mr. Downie, we now have that seat in business class you requested."

"But I didn't *ask* for a seat in business," I replied. Nerd, nerd, nerd, nerd, nerd.

On the other hand, the content of the work had me turning inward and slowly away from the demands and razzle-dazzle of the very medium which was making it possible. Television, a la *Man Alive*, was becoming the stick at the end of the carrot.

My experiences slowly showed me that the *institution* of the church in North America had become, in a way, more old-fashioned than wrong. Although it seemed to me that the energy of some communities was spent on a fairly vigorous hunt for scapegoats, in the end, evolution is no one's fault. I began to see how the inner life could be lived anywhere and fed outside the walls of a church, without losing any of the essential nature of the experience.

Man Alive also showed me how the church meant very different things to people in other parts of the world, which in turn meant, of course, that I saw how and why personal faith can also take on new dimensions.

A soft-spoken, studious, and middle-aged Jesuit philosopher from Canada demonstrated a courage of conviction by volunteering to go to El Salvador following the horrendous murders of six fellow Jesuits at their University of Central America, in San Salvador. We followed him there.

Michael Czerny, and five other volunteers – two Americans, two Spaniards and one Mexican – knew that to carry on the work of their slain colleagues and to live where they had died so violently was to be reminded daily, if not hourly, that there were good reasons to fear.

On a lovely, warm night with a gentle breeze, we went to the church where ten years before, a bullet had ripped through the heart of Archbishop Oscar Romero. I remember feeling uncomfortable about the nature of our job, in that place haunted by such un-gentle memories.

I think part of my discomfort lay in the fact that the *work* of television doesn't distinguish between events, and reduces everything to fit its particular appetite. So a discussion about lighting a refrigerator on the consumer program *Marketplace* is exactly the same as the discussion surrounding lighting the area where an assassination of an archbishop took place. I understood the mechanics. I just didn't like them much.

The violence in El Salvador during the ten-year period following Romero's murder was staggering. Estimates placed the number of dead as high as 71,000. It was still a place where violence or the threat of violence seemed always simmering just beneath the surface.

As we drove around and saw the army sandbagged and alert on every other street corner of San Salvador, my appreciation and curiosity about the force of Czerny's faith grew.

The campus of this private Jesuit university where Czerny now taught and lived had been an oasis of learning and a sanctuary from the ever-present civil war in El Salvador. But late one November night, as a guerrilla offensive brought the war from the countryside to the streets of San Salvador, all that had changed.

Heavily armed members of El Salvador's army, with blackened faces, went on a hate-filled, murderous, and drunken frenzy in the Jesuits' building. They shot through books of theology, and fired at and burned a picture of the late Archbishop Romero, who remained a powerful symbol, even in death.

Then, they escorted the six Jesuits from their beds, took them out back, forced them to lie on their stomachs on the grass, and quite literally blew their brains out.

University professors and priests were seen as the enemy in a country where dealing with the truth was dangerous. The symbolism of destroying the brains of these men was intended, as one human rights worker told me, to destroy the intellectual life of El Salvador.

There is a tall and lovely mango tree by the garden where the priests died. One night I stood in the silence of that strangely beautiful light which caresses the earth at dusk and tried to feel the terror of that horrible night six months before. How can anyone's faith survive when confronted by such heinous brutality? Part of the answer began to appear for me from an unlikely source.

His name is Abdullah Ramos, the gardener on the campus. And this night, when I stood staring at the still beauty of the mango tree, he quietly cared for the rose garden which, I learned, he had planted to honor the fallen priests.

What didn't receive the world-wide attention the murder of the priests had gained, was the tragedy that Ramos' wife, who worked as the Jesuits' housekeeper, and their 16-year-old daughter were in one of the small rooms in the priests' building the night of the attack.

I was shown photographs of what happened in that room. The chaos and destruction they depicted was so great that, at first, I couldn't even distinguish what I was looking at. When the twisted and broken bodies of Ramos' wife and daughter were pointed out, I felt like someone had kicked me in the stomach, and the blind, insane terror of that night became real.

The murder of the priests sent a political message. In a way, the vicious execution of these two women, whose only crime had been to be involved at the university, came to represent the 71,000 other civilians who had lost their lives in a war they could only suffer through.

And, as I watched this widower care for his new memorial garden on this serene evening, the nature of his faith also became real for me in a way I hadn't witnessed before.

I understood what the Jesuits represented and how important they still were, with honorable men like Michael Czerny ready to take up the fight. But I couldn't escape the idea that the exercise of faith for this gentle gardener, who had suffered such a personal loss, was in his gut, not in his head. It quite literally fed and nourished his soul, and he needed it to survive.

We followed Czerny to a small community in the countryside on the hottest day I have ever experienced. You should know that even holding a religious service qualified as a political statement and as an act of bravery in the El Salvador of this day. As routine a procedure as getting a map so we could find our way involved a military interrogation and search of our vehicle.

Czerny knew the importance of just being present in this town and that a large part of his task on this weekend was to help these poor people deal with the fear and the climate of persecution that was part of their daily life.

He accomplished much of that by simply showing up and was just as aware that when he left on this Sunday, people who took part in the service with him would pay for it during the coming week.

A member of their family might be picked up for questioning. They could just as easily become the subject of ugly rumors and innuendo in their close knit community. A threatening note could be nailed to their door. The military could pay them a visit for questioning.

The expression of faith for these poor people could carry with it a heavy price. These were lives diminished not only by poverty, but by suspicion and mistrust.

So the arrival of this shy Canadian and the other "replacement" priests sent a determined signal of perseverance, if not defiance. Czerny believed the commitment of the university community was to the truth, while their commitment as a Christian community and as priests was to the people, and he was willing, in his words, to "let the chips fall where they may."

Nowhere was that more evident than on this Sunday afternoon in this village. It was very moving to watch the simple joy of belief and the power of community come together. The optimism and strength felt as high as the sweltering humidity.

The dignity and openness of these people who welcomed strangers with smiles and generosity, sharing lemonade with us as friends, left an indelible impression on me. As did one of Czerny's questions.

"The point is, what do you live for?" It was a rhetorical question. But his answer was that if you live for something which is really worth living for, then you face a risk. "Life has to be risked in order to be lived fully."

That afternoon, witnessing something profound and essential in this remote place, I think I may have had the first inklings that I would no longer be able to remain detached from the stories I wanted to tell. And how in this small village, surrounded by proud peasants, flea-bitten dogs, and curious roosters, I felt a need to be closer to life than television would allow.

Needless to say, it all seemed light years away from the argument back home about whether gays should be admitted to congregations, and I left El Salvador with more perspective than I brought with me.

Back in Canada, I was meeting people – smart people who cared about meaning – who seemed to have at the very centre of their lives a set of convictions or values (I don't think *what* we call them is relevant) which gave them direction *without* identifying with or attending any church.

As we approach the end of this century, practically every major institution in our society is under attack and having to adapt itself to the new realities. It doesn't stand to reason that the church should be excluded from that questioning process.

The church, however, wasn't my major concern. The more I heard life's Big Questions and Answers played out by others in front of our cameras at *Man Alive*, the more I worried if, on television, we could do justice to the complexity of the situations in 28 minutes and 50 seconds.

Television compartmentalizes life into the tidy sections between commercials. As it becomes ever more dominant in our lives, it's little wonder we've lost our patience in the more challenging pursuit of faith.

This distinction is important for me. I think it's the *patience*, not the *appetite* we've lost. By relegating faith to a weekend activity like cutting the grass, we've largely stopped even attempting to blend it in more richly with our daily existence.

I was very, very lucky. Luckier, in fact, than I knew at the time. My "work" – in Matthew Fox's sense of the term, as discovering a place and role in the universe – and my "job" were blending together nicely. There was developing a valuable and interesting tension between my "job" of asking questions and my "work" of finding answers.

More and more, I found myself drawn to people who were, in one way or another, living their beliefs. Along the way, my appreciation for the complexity of faith was growing. I learned, for example, how demanding faith could be when it meant letting go, more than holding on.

All of this came together in the story I was most proud of doing during my time at *Man Alive*. The issues raised were far-reaching, but it most immediately involved a family living in Fort Fitzgerald, just on the border between Alberta and the Northwest Territories.

Let me back up a step to tell you how this came to be. For the past 15 years, on the first weekend in July, I have had the great pleasure of working with CBC broadcaster Katie Malloch and her *Jazzbeat* producer Alain de Grosbois on a "live" broadcast from the International Festival of Jazz in Montreal.

We've all been friends for a very long time and when I had to be away in Toronto with *Man Alive*, this weekend to get together with them became even more important to me. It was after the show one year when Katie told me the story of her sister Lesley and Lesley's husband Francois Paulette, who lived in "Fort Fitz," as it's called.

When I returned to Toronto and approached veteran producer F.M. Morrison with the idea, she jumped at it. And although Lesley and Francois were reluctant to go public for reasons you'll soon understand, they eventually agreed and we headed north.

At that time, Fort Fitzgerald boasted a population of 25, had no hydroelectric power, no running water, and no phone lines. Lesley and Francois lived with their only son, Thaidene, in a lovely rustic house, surrounded by a beautiful forest. It was a short, casual walk to the shores of the Great Slave River.

Francois had left his political activism behind when he quit being a Dene Chief, but he surely couldn't have imagined how native values would come to be at the heart of his family life after they had been blessed with a second son, whom they named K'aila.

It wasn't very long before Lesley noticed a bruise on K'aila's back, near his spine. She says now she had a premonition *then* that something was very wrong with their new son.

After many tests were conducted in Edmonton, Lesley and Francois were given the fearful news that K'aila had a fatal liver disease and the only way he would survive would be to undergo a liver transplant as quickly as possible. But Lesley and Francois didn't jump at the recommendation.

Lesley had a chance meeting with a nurse in Edmonton during one of her hospital stays there with K'aila. The nurse would tell her what the doctors had left out from their sales pitch. And that was that K'aila would be on enormously powerful antirejection drugs which, while saving his precious life, would at the same time make him more susceptible to all kinds of disease and infection for as long as he lived. She worried that they might save him now only to have him die from chicken pox at the age of 14.

Lesley returned home with K'aila, disturbed and uncertain about what they should do. Part of her uncertainty came from her belief that our physical being is intimately connected to our spiritual being. For Lesley, the implications of placing a body part into her son – the spirit from another soul – were disturbing.

She began to research and learn everything there was to know about the consequences of liver transplants. She discovered that not all doctors were as enthusiastic as those in Edmonton and concluded that, with the transplant, they would be turning baby K'aila's body into a war zone.

Francois believed that if the Creator had meant for us to place an organ from one body into another, then there would be no such war and no need for such drastic chemical measures to avoid rejection.

In one of the most powerful moments I've experienced on television, Lesley sat at her kitchen table and held out her hand, palm up.

She likened K'aila's birth to the landing of a beautifully-colored butterfly on her hand and she spoke softly of the choice before her at that precarious moment. She felt she could choose to enjoy the magnificent colors and spirit of this little visitor for as long as he wanted to stay resting on her hand, knowing that he could leave at any moment.

Or she could try to hold onto him by making a fist.

Lesley knew that by making a fist – by proceeding with the transplant – she would crumple her "butterfly's" beautiful wings and break his spirit.

And she wondered *who* this proposed transplant was really for, and whether their fear of losing K'aila was greater than the pain of doing what was right for him.

And so in the face of the advice from a well-intentioned doctor in Edmonton, and before the medical establishment's technological razzmatazz and intimidating power and influence, the couple, following their faith and convictions, decided that K'aila would not have the transplant. And that it was the right decision for *him*, though certainly not for themselves.

The doctor in Edmonton, guided by his own heart and set of beliefs, concluded that the parents were acting irresponsibly. He felt he had no choice but to refer the case to government authorities, eventually ending up with Alberta Social Services. The anguish was clear on Francois' face as he told me of the possibility of a helicopter landing at their home, with R.C.M.P. officers and government bureaucrats jumping out to seize their boy.

Lesley, Francois, and their increasingly sick son traveled – escaped – to Saskatchewan and found medical support there. But Alberta's authorities contacted those in Saskatchewan and the Paulettes found themselves in court having to defend what their beliefs had told them was the right thing to do.

After much legal and bureaucratic wrangling and the wasting of precious emotional and financial resources, the judge in Saskatchewan ruled in favor of Lesley, Francois, and K'aila. The family was now free to return home to Fort Fitzgerald. But K'aila never made it alive and died peacefully and quietly in Lesley's arms in Saskatchewan.

A ceremony was held in the woods behind their home and it is where K'aila now rests.

Like many people who wrote me following the broadcast, I'm almost positive I don't have the bravery to let go, to make the decision Lesley and Francois made. I was pleased and relieved that their initial fears of how their decision would be interpreted by the audience were unfounded. If anything, there was an understanding and heartfelt outpouring of support for them.

This episode of *Man Alive* went on to win numerous awards for so movingly showing the agonizing decisions taken by honest people, on all sides, wanting to do the right thing.

Its warm reception revealed three things to me. First, there's a deep hunger and desire for the serious discussion of the enormously complex issues facing all of us as we approach a new century. The march of technology is relentless and it is changing the way we live and are with each other. The sales pitch is all about what it can *do* for us – rarely about what it is *un*-doing.

The second thing I learned from the program on K'aila was a surprising one for me. It appeared that television was, in fact, quite capable of dealing with serious issues and conversations, although I confess I still wondered if there wasn't a more effective way and another place to conduct them.

Third, I was struck by how receptive people are, in fact, to the idea that a set of beliefs can direct life's most difficult decisions, even in the face of high-tech solutions and scientific promise.

Again, we're so driven by consumerism that the promise of technology to make everything better, faster, cheaper and quicker has been swallowed hook, line, and sinker, with little regard to consequences beyond personal ease and convenience.

Television is the giant electronic mouthpiece for this propaganda, which makes "A Choice for K'aila" and the subject matter it dealt with in prime time, stand out as the exception and not the rule for programming.

It was beginning to dawn on me that my view of faith, as existing at almost arm's length from daily concerns, might have been too narrow. And like the one good golf shot, or the one night – June 17, 1992, 7:34 p.m. – when the walleyes were biting, "A Choice for K'aila" filled me with a great enthusiasm and hope for my time at *Man Alive*.

ELEVEN

THE BREAKUP

Hope was emerging as an underlying theme in many of the stories I was hearing from people through *Man Alive*. And I still needed a wheelbarrow full of my own to carry me through the increasing moments of unease I had with television. I was learning to pick my spots and to live with some incredibly silly material on the program, but the creeping sense I had was that it wasn't going to get much better.

More and more, television was beginning to feel to me like lying to a good friend. There might be very good reasons for it, but at the end of the day, it doesn't make you feel any better or very good about it.

There were a million small things about the job and the medium which, separately, seemed almost nonsensical and quite manageable. But piled one on top of the other, they would have me up at 3:00 in the morning counting ulcers. Let me give you just a couple of quick examples.

While working on a program about facial disfigurement, I sat down to interview a guest who had started a group to help disfigured people cope with society's attitudes toward them. Before we began, the producer asked this guest to remove some make-up; the producer thought she "looked too good." Not disfigured enough.

In India, for the Child Haven story, I brought – carried in my arms, actually – a young girl who had been found abandoned on the doorstep of a nearby house. It was clear that if we wanted to show the promise and potential of a place like Child Haven, we'd have to tell the stories of where some of these kids had come from.

We carefully and fully discussed whether it was proper to bring this little girl back to that neighborhood and to subject her to whatever memories might still haunt her. With the permission of those who knew her better than us, we decided to return, with her, to where she was found.

The producer had decided to use an Indian crew for this shoot: first, to save money, and second, because they would enable us to move about that society more freely and in a more inconspicuous way. This was one night I wish we had used an Indian host.

Our crew could blend in to the point of disappearance on the street. That was no problem. But a fairly large white man carrying a tiny Indian girl in his arms through an impossibly crowded neighborhood gathers unwanted attention. As we approached the place where she had been found, I could feel her body tense in my arms and she began to visibly shake with each step that brought us closer.

I couldn't believe what I was doing to this poor, frightened youngster, just so we could get a ten-second television shot. And it wasn't going to be only one trip to where she'd been found. We'd need shots from all angles to be able to use this sequence, which meant subjecting her (and me) to the same thing over and over and over again. In the end, we stopped and never used her story as part of ours.

Technically and even creatively, television demands that certain basic things be taken care of, but when you're dealing with only one camera, these various shots can take forever. I know it is important and necessary, but it leaves little room for people's feelings and none for spontaneity whatsoever. In my mind, television's "end" was increasingly less able to justify the "means" to get there. I just didn't have it in me to put up with it all after awhile.

It seemed to me we were always just tip-toeing back and forth across the fine line between truth and deception – a little time spent on each side, but rarely ever managing to balance on it.

After a visit to Vancouver Island, where we visited the hermit priest Father Charles Brandt and shot him fly-fishing in the Oyster River by his hermitage, I was yanked away by another producer. It was a few weeks before I saw the fly-fishing footage when I returned.

Something didn't look right about it, but I couldn't put my finger on what had changed. It turned out the producer had "colorized" the forest to make it look greener than it had *actually* been in the winter, when we had *actually* been there.

I don't mean in the Ted Turner kind of total colorization of old movies. This was more a subtle shading of the forest, and the truth. Why in the world, I wondered, would this producer play around with something as natural and lovely as a forest on Vancouver Island at any time of the year?

The answer is ridiculously Sir Edmund Hillary-like. This producer used the technology because it was there and because he could. And isn't that the way of most technology and our relationship to it? On my television set, there's a button I can push to freeze the image on the screen while the audio portion of the program proceeds. Who uses that? For what? This function is there only because somebody figured out how to do it.

In a conversation with Neil Postman, we talked about the impact of technology and how we are often unaware of a hidden consequence. As an example, he cited the invention of eyeglasses. When they were first introduced, they seemed miraculous, and who could argue that they helped thousands of people to see better?

But the profound, underlying message introduced into the culture was that the work of God (or whatever term you're comfortable with) could be improved upon by mere mortals. The consequences of something as apparently simple as a pair of eyeglasses can be far-reaching and hidden from most of us.

Like the eyeglasses, television carries with it some beneficial results, but I don't think we've even begun to understand how damaging and corrosive it has been to the human spirit and how it has ripped through the human community like a violent tornado.

Technology creates this artificial need and then bursts on the scene with solutions to problems we weren't having. Where radio lives solely by ideas, emotion, and atmosphere, television is completely driven and consumed by and subservient to its technology. Every time a new gimmick becomes available, we feel it has to be used, regardless of its value.

Now, by itself, I don't think adding a little green to the forest is really a major reason to get upset or to throw in the towel, but about the only thing I ever took very seriously was my reputation. I always did my best to be as straight and honest as I could be in presenting material.

As it was my face and my credibility attached to these stories, even this little bit of harmless sneakiness revealed to me a manipulative mentality I didn't much care for. As Arlo Guthrie and Pete Seeger sang once about Richard Nixon's cries of ignorance surrounding the activity of his cohorts, "Well, then, what else didn't he know?"

The comparison is particularly apt in the case of one particular producer. I would find out in a subsequent program, after the fact unfortunately, that he deliberately misled me and in turn, you, by presenting a guest he knew was lying. This was not the stretching or exaggeration of truth. This guest told outright lies which served this producer's purpose, and that's all that mattered to him.

I told a senior producer about this, and nothing was done. Not a damn thing happened. Think about that and you'll understand why my enthusiasm to work with this bunch was fading.

The contradiction between what *Man Alive* was supposed to be about and how it operated was more apparent and troubling to me the longer I stayed there. This meant there were times I looked the other way when it came to process; I just kept my head down, concentrating only on my contribution to the final product.

This was not difficult. Especially when I could spend time with men like Father Charles Brandt on Vancouver Island, who exemplified the hope and personal conviction I increasingly sought.

Father Brandt is the only person in 200 years to be ordained by the Catholic Church as a hermit, and although that's *what* he is, it doesn't come close to explaining *who* he is.

Father Brandt saw an intimate connection between being a priest and an avid fly-fisherman and environmentalist, and he spoke to me with such hope and optimism about the transformation of human hearts and minds, all leading to a new vision of our place in the universe, that it was hard to argue with him. Even had I wanted to.

For as long as I can remember, the natural world has been vitally important to my inner sense of well-being and ability to cope with the concrete world. Part of the attraction for me in nature is that it simply *is* – period. There is an air of grace about the natural world that calls me to it.

As I'm regularly accused of being a hermit, I was most anxious to meet a "real" one and felt a kinship with Brandt before even arriving at his comfortable hermitage.

I was beginning to hear a kind of confirming language from people like Brandt, whose words encouraged and reassured me about the direction I seemed to be drawn in, all the while, in effect, inviting me away from the world of television and the media.

I know that if you don't believe in this kind of stuff, then hearing someone – even someone as learned as Father Brandt – talk of the trees and animals and rivers and flowers as having a language of *their* own, you're going to think he's at least one bubble off level.

But in my case, he was talking to the converted. As he was when he said that nature's conversation was ours to hear, if we'd only stop being so caught up in ourselves. Asking television people to stop being caught up in themselves is like asking the fish to just relax and enjoy the boat ride.

Brandt's way of not getting caught up in himself was through meditation, which he characterized as an "assault against the ego." The stillness of meditation and the action-hungry television camera are simply not a great mix. I can hear the comment now, "Well, is he going to move or anything?"

Brandt believed that only through keeping the always-present ego in its place could a communion with the natural world be achieved.

And that's how he felt about his cherished fly-fishing on the Oyster River. It was a way for him to stay in touch with Earth's creatures. Try telling *that* to the boss the next time you skip an afternoon to get out on the lake. Let me know how you make out.

For Father Brandt, fly-fishing constantly reminded him, he said, that everything out there is a "community of subjects, not a collection of objects."

I was struck by the phrase and knew the sentiment was close to my heart and as far away from the reality of television work as imaginable. I believed him when he said the route to this awareness was through meditation and silence. This contemplative tradition in the Christian church dates back thousands of years. The contemplative tradition of television stretches back to last Wednesday.

He spoke of how humans had turned away from and stopped believing in the goodness of the earth around the time of the plague or black death which decimated a third of Europe's population.

It was believed that God was angry and was punishing the world. Up until that point, the earth had been seen by people as largely revelatory – that humanity, nature, and the earth were combined as one sacred community.

I still remember a phrase he used about the modern environmental movement and how the confrontational aspects of it would end as we got further and further into what he described as a new "age of the earth."

He said that we had all been "terrorized by a lack of hope," and that through a more contemplative life, we'd come to understand fully the old Cartesian saying, "never less alone than when alone." I left Father Brandt, wanting to stay and fish and talk with him into the night.

And that was becoming an occupational hazard, representing perfectly the dilemma when one's work meets one's job. While there were some guests I couldn't wait to get away from – look for the next book – I was meeting more and more whom I didn't want to leave.

The great mixed curse of working on a program like *Man Alive* was that television kept rearing its ugly head and I always had to return to the real world.

This leads me to think of Jean Vanier, who in some ways left that real world in the mid-'60s to build his l'Arche community in the pastoral beauty of the French countryside. It has now grown into something like 95 communities, operating in 22 countries around the world.

We were working on *Man Alive*'s 25th anniversary show, and even for people as accustomed to weird hours and loads of travel as we were, the schedule was ridiculous. We had been on the east coast, then through New Mexico and California, ended up working in New York on a Friday, then flew to Paris, drove north and visited Vanier and l'Arche, and were home Monday night.

But even in such a short visit, it was impossible not to be touched by the members of that community, and by Vanier himself, again. Our paths had crossed before, so I knew something of the eloquence he would muster in discussing how, in our competitive society and in our blind celebration of power, we push down the weak. And how, when we elevate money and prestige above everything else, we end up killing a part of our being.

This was exactly how I was feeling, even though I couldn't have found, then, the appropriate language to describe it. This great change in my life – hosting *Man Alive*, with all its accompanying attention and benefits – was so easy, and happened so quietly, that I never quite realized what I had lost.

Outwardly, I had more of everything our society values. On its terms, I was certainly successful; I made a lot of money and even my limited celebrity generally ensured that strangers would treat me kindly, if not with favors.

So why did I feel empty inside? Like the growl of a hungry stomach, my spirit wanted food and wouldn't let me go very long without reminding me of its condition. I could and did mask this kind of nagging inner hunger by collecting possessions, which came to perform a kind of reassuring role in my life.

The power of society's perceptions and our desire to be "seen" as achieving a status within it are such that it makes it remarkably easy to ignore the inner voice. Our culture, mainly through television, turns us away from ourselves by presenting models and situations which require little thought or questioning.

"Not thinking" is exactly what those who have power in our society want. The values elevated all around us have nothing to do with how we treat our inner self, or how we behave toward and with each other, and yet those concerns were taking up more and more of my time away from "the job."

In a way, this emptiness I felt only grew the more I supposedly achieved, as measured by the standards all around me. So it was truly a delight to see Jean Vanier again and to meet all the people in that community. As it happened, we were there for his birthday party. What a touching and loving celebration it was.

We all formed a kind of circle around Vanier in this large garden setting, and watched as the mentally disabled members of the community, with sheer joy and love bursting from their happy faces, couldn't wait for their turn to go to the centre and embrace this man, their friend who truly knew and cared for them.

Vanier was still as critical then of our embrace of so-called progress, and all the materialist baggage that "progress" brings with it, as he was over 30 years ago. And like Father Brandt, here was someone else directing me inward, giving me the strength and, almost, the permission to join that inner battle.

Vanier has always said we will only discover who we truly are through the brotherhood and sisterhood of community. I can still see his gentle face smiling as he said most of us don't even know what community is about anymore, that we tend to think of it as an area of the city.

What he means by community is a caring and a bonding that leads to openness and a feeling of belonging which, he pointed out, so few of us have experienced. He spoke passionately, as we sat in his small room, about how we were all conceived for communion, in essence the to and fro of love.

And according to Vanier, to love someone is not an emotional or sentimental exercise. It is, in his words, "to reveal to the other person their beauty, to reveal the light inside them which tells them they are a living being."

We spent our last night at l'Arche in a large room with lots of singing and laughter. When we said goodbye, I confessed to Vanier that while acknowledging the power of what I had seen happening around me, I didn't feel yet that I quite understood it. He sort of chuckled, put his hand on my shoulder, and said "Then, come and live with us." If he'd only known ...

Within hours, the real world was all too real. The soundman and I, racing to return the van at the airport in Paris, managed to somehow get it wedged between the ceiling of the underground parking area and the road surface of a ramp we shouldn't have taken.

We abandoned the van and breathlessly raced to the check-in counter. Within seconds, there was a very loud and public screaming match between the cameraman and said soundman about the packing of certain equipment.

As I stood there watching this unfold before me, the words of Vanier returned: "One of the gifts of l'Arche is that we see how much we need each other."

Even as I watched this shouting match, I still believed what Vanier had said. I was beginning, though, to think that this power to change, this desire for inner survival, also had to come from the "inside."

It was fine and even instructive to hear the words from people like Vanier and Brandt, but the task before me was to find my own words and to *live* them for it all to really mean anything.

This frenzied business of television, which at its very best can only pretend to capture life, was, at the same time, offering challenging pieces of a puzzle I wanted to work on.

Community. Faith. Love. Courage. Hope. These were the words I heard expressed again and again in conversations with guests. I took them seriously. It struck me as well that, more and more, people were reflecting on the need to get closer to the earth, to care in a profound way for this big blue ball floating through space.

218 | PETER DOWNIE

This idea of hope and a relationship with the earth which Father Brandt had expressed on Vancouver Island would surface again in a memorable conversation I had in a penthouse suite in London, England. After a day of talking, we stood on the balcony watching the Concord circle London, heading for a landing.

Beside me, and every bit as entranced by the sight of this distinctive prehistoric bird-like aircraft, was 84-year-old Sir Laurens van der Post, a man whose thoughts and perspective on life edged me ever closer to getting as far away from television as I could.

When I heard that he had died recently, I smiled at the thought of his adventuresome spirit and wondered if he had yet managed to hook up with his old friend Carl Jung on an entirely different kind of plane. He believed he would.

In case you are unaware of Sir Laurens, let me take a second to give you a very quick biographical sketch. He was born in South Africa and remained connected to the spirit of the bushmen of the Kalahari, whom he profiled in 1956 with his celebrated television special called *In Search of The Lost World of Kalahari*. At the time it was hailed as an anthropological epic.

In 1939, he was a private in the British army and only two years later, he was leading a commando unit against the Japanese in Java, where, like thousands of others, he was taken prisoner.

Not only did he face, daily, the prospect of his own death, he was forced to watch daily executions of his men. His experiences as a Japanese prisoner of war inspired the film starring David Bowie called *Merry Christmas Mr. Lawrence*.

During his rich life he wrote 20 books, which sold millions around the world. He had celebrated friendships with figures such as T.S. Eliot, Lord Mountbatten, and as mentioned, the Swiss psychoanalyst Carl Jung.

What I said in the simple introduction of that episode might even be more true today than it was then. "This is one of the most remarkable men of our time, with a simple message of hope."

At the time of his death, Sir Laurens was godfather to Prince Charles and Diana's eldest son William, and had been known to consult with the Prince and Margaret Thatcher on occasion. As much as he hated it, he was regularly referred to as the Prince's spiritual mentor by the dreaded English tabloids.

It was a relationship neither ever spoke of publicly, so I was left to only admire Charles' watercolors which graced Sir Laurens' sitting room. It is hard to tell you what it was like to be in this man's presence, but I think when you hear what he had to say, you'll understand the impact it had on me.

It's one of only two *Man Alive* programs I've ever watched again, and even though it was shot beautifully by the very gifted cameraman Steve Adamcryck, television can't capture what it was like to sit with Sir Laurens.

I felt as if I was before a great and kind and even gentle wisdom which seemed to understand the world in a way not many do. Unlike Father Charles Brandt before him, Sir Laurens wasn't particularly hopeful. He predicted that we might have only 100 years left to change our ways and our relationship to the planet.

One of his qualities which I enjoyed most was the value he placed on real experience. He claimed he didn't need university professors to tell him of the destruction of the earth. In his lifetime, he said sadly, he had seen plenty with his own eyes.

But he spoke of the earth and the water and the air and the clouds and the grass and all creatures with such loving attention, that it seemed absolutely natural for him to call this planet "a jewel." I've often thought of a conversation he said he had just had with an Indian from the rain forest, in his apartment the day before we arrived.

Following another violent and damaging wind storm across the British Isles, this Indian asked Sir Laurens why no one listened to the wind. He believed the wind carried with it great messages, if only we would hear them.

And Sir Laurens used a phrase I'll never forget when he said we're living in a "Tower of Babel moment," where – forget the wind – even *people* aren't hearing each other anymore. We recognize the sounds of speech, but we miss the meaning.

It isn't *information* we are lacking, said Sir Laurens, it's the sense of going somewhere with the spirit and imagination that is absent from our lives. He told me that what the spirit can't stand is a life without meaning and said that most of us, when we lie down at night in the dark, feel increasingly lost in the universe.

I remember sitting there so mesmerized by this frail man, with his watery blue eyes that seemed to reflect the oceans of the world, that I almost forgot to ask any questions.

He spoke of the "comfortable disease of progress" where we forget about entering into a partnership with time and treat it only as something to be beaten. He pointed out that in all the world's mythologies, humanity is warned against making haste. "Why the hurry?" he wondered.

He talked of our "little memory," that is, the time since our birth, then of the "great memory," of all creation and our place in it. He said, "Even when we forget it, it goes on remembering us." Hope filled the television screen.

When he had been a prisoner of war held by the Japanese, he said he knew the men felt like the continuity of their lives had been broken by being in prison. But Sir Laurens wrote them all a letter saying this brokenness was only an illusion and that the continuity of life was still there within each of them.

He established school and university courses in prison, handing out degrees written on lavatory paper. He came to realize that "our most difficult problems are our most precious possessions because they are the raw material of our fulfillment and of our redemption."

When I did remember to stop listening and to ask a question, it had to do with the idea that modern societies make us all feel imprisoned in one way or another. I was delighted when he agreed quickly and pointed out that this condition was precisely why it was critical for all of us to care for our inner climate as much as for the external climate of our planet.

As he went on to say, the external climate is what conditions the rain and brings on the wind. Our internal climate is realized through our dreams and our mythologies, and is an integral part of our existence. He said we should follow our longings and our wantings, even if our desire was to raise chickens or sing or draw, and he predicted the joy would return and the world would be changed.

In a previous chapter, I mentioned my growing sense that what is essential in life remains invisible, and Sir Laurens was saying things that powerfully reinforced that idea. "It is not in the great plans or grand schemes and cathedrals that the change will come," he said as we closed the interview. "It will come in the hearts of ordinary people by finding the cathedral in themselves." This was a call to action, or so it seemed to these ears.

He said all of this and much more in such an understanding and compassionate way that it inspired in me the desire for something more out of my life. I know, theoretically, that's not supposed to happen in these situations, but I can't tell you how many times the words of this wise man have come back to me in recent years.

What I can tell you, without pride or satisfaction, is that it was a real struggle to get this episode on the air. Conventional wisdom at *Man Alive* when I left was that viewers will pay attention for 3.2 seconds before switching the channel. Probably even less now.

I think that's insulting nonsense, but then again, it wasn't my call. I was astonished to hear Sir Laurens van der Post dismissed as a talking head which no one would watch. This, from *Man Alive*, the one program which should have welcomed him. In fact, I received almost as much response from "The Last Dreamer" as I had for the earlier broadcast of "A Choice for K'aila."

But audience figures are like all other statistics and can quite easily be manipulated to support the argument of the person holding them. There's no doubt we were all certainly talking about ratings far more when I left *Man Alive* than when I had first arrived.

In the same way that it was surprising to discover that Gorbachev somehow didn't realize that the Soviet Union was held together only by fear, the old gang at *Man Alive* seemed to have forgotten what made the program special, what allowed it to be above the usual television fray.

The integrity of *Man Alive* was crumbling like the Berlin Wall and vanishing like the old borders of the Soviet Union.

It *had* been the one program on television where *conversation* with provocative thinkers was allowed to happen in as natural a way as was possible, given the medium. But it was the *ideas* which attracted viewers, not the artsy shot of a burning candle, or a close-up of a tear streaming down someone's cheek.

All television chasing audience figures and advertising dollars is infected with this kind of pretentious and cheap emotional manipulation, and now on the public network, *Man Alive* was following suit. In this climate, a provocative thinker became a boring "talking head." Simple, direct, good conversation wouldn't leave the producer with enough to play with, taking too much control from his or her hands.

The art of conversation and the beauty of ideas don't need to be artificially jazzed up. The very second *Man Alive* turned away from its unique character, I think it started to lose its way. Sexual abuse, alien abductions, abandoned children, sex change operations. This was the kind of sensational stuff increasingly raised at story meetings.

During the making of the 25th anniversary show, I saw how far the program had slipped. The kinds of thinkers who used to be the regular fare were no longer welcome, as *Man Alive* slowly became like so many other tabloid productions.

At its heart, this brand of editorial thinking signified the triumph of the lowest common denominator and regarded the audience as dupes. A kind of pseudo-intellectual arrogance was becoming suffocating at *Man Alive* and I regretfully began to wonder what I could do next.

It was a hard decision to make, because I think some of the best work was still to come as the producers and I became more comfortable with each other. But the emptiness was growing inside me and an experience I had had with the Dalai Lama came back to mind and helped me find my way to the answer which felt right.

I had spent some time with him in Los Angeles and was told, before leaving Toronto, that this most revered religious and exiled civil leader of Tibet absolutely loved electronic and technological gadgets of all kinds.

As I had just purchased one of these modern, intricately complex 35 mm cameras equipped with all the latest bells and whistles, I thought he might like to see it. In any case, I told myself, it could serve as an ice-breaker between us – which showed how little I knew of this man.

I discovered immediately that there is no ice around the Dalai Lama, and while the impact of being with him in a room was not as great as I had been warned by a few of his followers, it was still for me a tremendously powerful experience.

I must declare here, with less pride than once accompanied this fact, that I was, am, and likely will for evermore be a technological Luddite. Considering that, I spent the better part of the flight to Los Angeles reading and re-reading the information about this completely automated photographic marvel I held in my hands.

When I wasn't poring over the manual on the way to Los Angeles, I was thinking about the "warnings" I had received concerning what it was like to be in the presence of the Dalai Lama.

I had never had a convincing mystical experience of my own, although there were a couple of chemically-induced situations at university that came close. But that was a long time ago and so I sort of hoped something magical would happen when I met him. And in its own unexpected and delayed way, it did.

Back to the camera for a moment. By the time we landed, I was confident that I would be able to, at least, go over its impressive specifications, and with a few highlights of its many high-tech functions thrown in, I was ready – provided he didn't ask many questions.

It was one of those absolutely perfect afternoons on the Pacific coast – soaked to the point of dripping in sunshine and stroked by a gentle, massaging breeze – when I sat down with the Dalai Lama in a Santa Monica apartment overlooking the sparkling diamond surface of the Pacific Ocean.

The floor of the room was covered with the brightly-colored crimson and gold robed bodies of monks, whose gaze upward at the Dalai Lama reminded me of nothing as much as my sunflower garden at home. These devoted monks seemed to crane their necks to be closer to their own source of warmth and life.

As our talk finished and the dreary business of television had to be taken care of, I brought my camera out and with a measure of confidence, launched into my much rehearsed explanation of this technological wonder. He listened patiently and attentively and when I was done, I handed him the camera to hold and look through.

Without missing a beat, he asked the one question I wasn't ready to answer. In fact, it was one I hadn't even considered.

The Dalai Lama smiled and asked, "Does it take good pictures?"

The absurdity of all my preparation and his intuitive, instant grasp of the essential had us all laughing with an ease and familiarity that erased the fact we were strangers. It was as if the Dalai Lama had raised some kind of cosmic curtain, for a second revealing the silliness of the universe exactly as Toto had exposed the truth about the Wizard of Oz.

It was a very valuable lesson to me to keep my eye on the fundamentals of a situation and to have in mind, always, the over-riding question of purpose. In turn, this meant that I began to question – with some intention now – the role of the media in our lives, but more specifically in mine.

On the flight home from Los Angeles, it occurred to me that all my consumption on the earn and spend merry-go-round, all my material possessions, all the fights at work over nonsense, all my ambitions and flights of ego, and all my fears and insecurities were nothing but the equivalent of my camera's bells and whistles.

None of it had anything to do with finding a picture from the developing fluid of a life. I was, at once, energized and frightened by the question and the possibilities.

TWELVE

"AH ... YOU'LL GET OVER IT"

While I was getting more involved with some of the guests from *Man Alive*, I found out I was feeling increasingly removed from the process. Part of that, I think, was simply the result of the nature of work on a documentary series, and part of it was clearly the way the program was administered.

In any event, many of the exchanges with guests were staying with me longer and in such a personal way that they were coming to mean more to me than they should have in a journalistic context, more than during all the years of programs I had worked on before.

Let me give you one small example. We were working at the southernmost tip of Bangladesh on a program about a couple of Canadian doctors with the group *Medecins sans Frontieres*, or Doctors Without Borders.

There had been a massive exodus of Muslims from Myanmar, escaping persecution across the Bay of Bengal. Thousands upon thousands of these refugees were crammed into camps in the south and had become a real and growing headache to the government of Bangladesh.

Essentially, they had overstayed their welcome, and yet the idea of forcing them out was unthinkable, if only logistically. One afternoon we stood in the middle of one of these camps, drawing a crowd with the television camera in the way I imagine snake oil salesmen once did in early North American frontiers. Someone came up beside me, pushed a piece of crumpled up paper in my hand, and melted into the crowd.

Later that night, I uncrumpled it and read the message. It now hangs on the wall in my office as a daily reminder. Here it is, exactly as written in purple crayon:

> Every day Dhoapalong camp officers called some
> refugees. Camp officers told them and post that
> you must go your country. Refugees don't agree to
> their country with out demand. After then the
> camp officers heardly beat them and then police
> said if you do not go back to your own country
> I will send you to jail. They forst refugees
> to go back roughly yesterday. They sent at least
> 100 refugees roughly.
> If you kind us you better come to our
> Dhoapalong refugees camp and see.
> – Dhoapalong refugees

It is a powerful reminder to me that there are millions of souls in this world without influence, displaced, dishonored, and forced to live with crushed spirits and little hope.

I think my work was becoming more assured on the program and that the producers and I had arrived, if not on the same page, then at least at the point of circling each other in the same library. The result of all this was that I could get beyond the mechanics and pay more attention to the actual content with a new confidence in the material.

I was also learning how important it was to have the buoyancy of that confidence in the deep waters sometimes offered by *Man Alive*. As with so many new or difficult experiences in life, the willingness to admit "I don't know," coupled with an honest intention, is more than half the battle.

It is tricky business finding the right language to use in speaking about such an intensely private part of one's life. It doesn't help that our culture devalues expressions of faith or that television eats modesty for breakfast.

Here again was a curious contradiction. The language around this whole area of faith and belief has become so burdened and heavy with baggage, I found it almost impossible to approach the path to, say, the subject of God, without having to first fend my way through an overgrown jungle of stale animosities and fresh angers.

And yet, I was discovering that almost everyone, except of course most journalists who were far too smart to fall for any of this, was seeking with an honest and honorable desire something more in their life. I'm afraid I wasn't as smart as most journalists and so was forced to join the great unwashed hungry proletariat in this journey.

It was almost certain that this wasn't an exploration to be conducted within the boundaries of traditional religion or within the walls of mainstream churches, and while there may be reasons to regret that, it in no way diminished the intensity of the search.

The shape of our bodies had become more important than

the fitness of our inner life and I was discovering a real hunger for a kind of spiritual workout.

I wasn't as sure that television was the place this could be carried out, and as I was mulling all of this over, I met a man who reminded me of the time, almost 20 years before, when I first set out on this track.

Just weeks before he died, Dr. Robert McClure was, as the title of the episode so accurately called him, "irrepressible."

When he first appeared on CBC television in 1966, it was suggested that he was nearing the end of the trail. He had, after all, reached the ripe old age of 65, when many of his generation were taking retirement and slowing down.

Five years after that, Dr. McClure appeared on *Man Alive* and said he hoped somebody would tell him when "there was no tread left on my tires."

In the late summer of 1991, I met an almost 91-year-old McClure who still had plenty of "rubber" to burn. Even though he spoke with such passionate conviction and enthusiasm, it was still a bit surprising when he almost barked at me that "I have a call. I was put on earth to do something. I wasn't just an accident of a sperm meeting an ovum on a dark night."

It was impossible not to smile at his crustiness or to wonder at his optimism. Here was a missionary doctor who had practiced surgery in China in the '20s, in India in the '50s, and in the '70s, following a sometimes controversial stint as the first lay moderator of the United Church of Canada, in North Borneo and Zaire.

When we met, he was still out raising hell and money for Third World medicine, which had been such a large part of his life. But he was not one to sit and ruminate on the past. Each experience was now a closed chapter, he said.

He would speak to anyone, but especially to students, in a tough, unsentimental, and pragmatic way. We followed him to a classroom one afternoon where he told the students straight out they wouldn't get anywhere by "sitting on their butts staring at the sky."

It was clear that this current chapter of life – as it turned out, his last chapter – was to be spent convincing young people that they were here on earth for a reason. He wanted them to hear "a calling," to embrace the idea that they had to do something in a world which was getting ever smaller.

It was the Third World which kept calling McClure back. He had tried practicing medicine in Canada, but didn't feel busy enough doing only two major surgeries a week. As he told me proudly, in these so-called Third World nations, he'd do 85 operations a week, 60 of which would be major.

As I stood in the back of this classroom in Toronto watching McClure, I realized suddenly that everything he was saying applied to me as much as to the students. As if I had done something embarrassing, I quickly looked around to see if anyone had noticed.

The very strong and certain "calling" I heard as a young man in New Brunswick had pretty much run its course and, to be honest, the thought terrified me. I knew I was becoming increasingly interested in matters of the human spirit, but the course wasn't nearly as defined or clear as it had been back in 1970. This time it didn't have the irresistible force of what McClure referred to as a "calling."

What it *did* have, and what was missing from that by-now ancient calling of mine, was the idea and ideal of relationship, that it was critical to stay engaged in all ways with the world. To this day, it remains the greatest gift from *Man Alive*.

Although I was still in an industry that demanded lots of ego, I wasn't satisfied anymore with it being about me. I was, already, internally giving myself the hook. A painful exercise.

So with one foot out and my heart hooked up to a new and private journey, I continued hosting *Man Alive* and meeting people who unwittingly were now providing little signposts along this new path of mine.

Canadian Dr. Chris Giannou, for example, had been in the most troubled spots of the world, like McClure, practicing medicine and, inevitably, politics.

When we got together in Canada, he had most recently been in Beirut with the Palestinian Red Crescent Society, working under the most extreme conditions of refugee camps under fire. He clearly loved every adrenalin-packed second of it.

His eyes would virtually sparkle when describing the contribution he could make to the health and well-being of the mainly forgotten people around the world, victims caught up in ugly and brutal wars.

Giannou used a phrase in our conversation which I never forgot. We were talking about his sense of home considering how nomadic his life had been. He said that home for him was not a geographic space, but a moral one. And like so many others on *Man Alive* who perhaps used different language, Giannou was talking about a life of *responsibility*.

I had almost given up hoping for responsibility from television, but it felt only natural to continue wondering about mine. I was coming into contact with people who only encouraged me to carry on in that direction.

I spent a little time with the psychologist and Pulitzer Prize-winning writer and Harvard professor Dr. Robert Coles, when we went to speak with him about his latest book, *The Spiritual Life of Children*. He believed children to be "works of art. If not God's, then nature's." I found him to be an enormously likable and decent man.

As a young doctor in the '50s, he found himself treating the last generation of children stricken by polio before the arrival of the Salk vaccine. In ways that would deeply affect and direct his life, Coles listened to the introspection of children about suffering and illness and the possibility of death.

One young man and patient whom Coles recalled was a basketball player, only a couple of years younger than he was at the time, lying in bed with two useless legs. This man about Coles' age said to him once, "You should get down on your knees and thank God that you can walk. You should get down on your knees and thank God that you're well."

Then came the '60s and the civil rights battles, including desegregation, in the American south. This was when a six-year-old black student named Ruby Bridges faced jeering, angry mobs day after day in New Orleans.

On one of those days, Bob Coles just happened to be driving by the school and saw Ruby all alone against the crowd. He was struck by her calmness and courage before a crowd which wanted to kill her.

Ruby and her family would enter his heart and change his life, offering, as he put it, "the chance to learn more about ourselves. Frightened, desperate, harassed black people, in great jeopardy, could teach me a lot as I saw their strengths unfold and their dignity become quite apparent to everyone."

234 | PETER DOWNIE

Coles believed that this little girl's sorrowful vulnerability highlighted how he and others who happened to be more fortunate could be guilty of strutting and showing off. I wondered at this point if, in addition to his psychological work, Coles was a mind reader.

After he came to know Ruby and her family, Coles spoke of first being interested, then intrigued, and finally "committed to something." That commitment was to work with very poor and vulnerable people in a climate of segregation, "where basically they had no access to white doctors."

Bob Coles used slightly different language, but he was talking about the same thing as McClure's "calling," Sir Laurens van der Post's "inner cathedral," Chris Giannou's "moral space," Jean Vanier's "gift of needing each other at l'Arche," and Father Brandt's awareness that we are, in this life, a "community of subjects, not a collection of objects."

Coles' commitment has meant a lifetime of considering and struggling with achievement versus conduct. After attaining objects which our society values – a medical degree for example – how do we make sure, he wondered, that we go on to behave in an honorable and decent way?

"This," he said, "was the biggest challenge to any of us." It had certainly become that for me.

In one of his lectures we attended, he asked the privileged students of Harvard, "Where's the truth? Where's the language that will even help us with the truth? Is it going to come out of the mouths of those senators whose very living depends on the mouthing of pieties that say nothing?"

Coles teaches one of the most popular courses at Harvard, The Literature of Social Reflection. He is determined that these slightly older children learn that one can succeed at school, but fail at life. We do well to remember that we are, in his words, "all pilgrims slouching toward Bethlehem."

As we sat in his office at home on a perfect New England fall day, Dr. Coles handed me a profound and completely unintentional revelation. Maybe the best kind.

We were making what was usually small talk as everything was being set up. He had worked for Robert Kennedy and became quite emotional when remembering the loss and what it had taken from his life.

In many ways, I think it was the last time he had been passionately engaged by politics, and the absence of that still seemed very real to him. I stumbled over the words trying to find a way to express my sentiments to him. I said something like, "I'm always surprised by life and how ..." and let it just trail off, as the crew scurried around us. He finished the sentence for me.

"Disappointing it is," he said with a smile.

It may not seem like much to you reading those words, and maybe they even strike you as trite. And I could pretend to be smarter and more detached as a journalist by saying they were obvious to me, but they weren't.

I felt in my heart, at that moment, what it was that had been the engine of my restlessness, driving my search for something more. I wanted not to be disappointed by life. It couldn't have been any simpler.

The Dalai Lama and his wonderful question, "Does it take good pictures?" ran through my mind as I just stared for a second at Dr. Coles, trying to catch my breath and weighing the option of lunging across and hugging him.

I didn't. It wasn't the time or place to burst and although we have exchanged books and correspondence since, I've never been able to tell him of that moment and all that his three wise and well-chosen words meant to me.

Dr. Coles took me out for a spin in his 30-year-old Porsche and as we whipped through the brightly colored leaves on winding New England roads, it was another grand day where I loved what I was working on, but not what I did.

With added intellectual fuel from Dr. Coles, I increased my wondering about what it meant to be successful. Although I had all the trappings of success, I didn't feel truly *connected* to very much. The idea that just being aware could be the first small step toward a new definition of success was never far from my mind. This awareness was not an easy one to absorb, given the throw-away culture of my job.

I felt that a hungry child, anywhere in the world, was mine, that any abused and lonely senior was a member of my family, and that my responsibility as a human being was to give a voice to the oppressed, exploited, frightened, and silenced souls of this world. I never want to learn to limit my goals.

I made up my mind to leave *Man Alive* after one specific interview, and not because it was dreadful. I knew by then that as far as viewers were concerned, those didn't happen anymore. If some conversation was awful – this of course is only hypothetical – the crew, the producer, the editor and I were the only ones to know, as it hit the editing room floor.

No, the contradiction is that, as odd as this is going to sound, I decided to leave because something "worked" extremely well, in television terms. It was that those were terms I was no longer able to live with, similar to not wanting to belong to any club which would have me as a member. I just knew I couldn't pretend any longer.

We were in Los Angeles to interview Elizabeth Bouvia, a name which might be familiar to you. In the '80s, Elizabeth, who suffers from advanced cerebral palsy, severe arthritis and scoliosis, had gone to court in California to win the right to starve herself to death. That's right – another cheery 30-minute television program.

She lost and was now on such a strong morphine drip directly into her heart that starvation would apparently be far too painful for her to carry out. She said she still wanted to die.

It was hard to blame her. She had been confined to a small hospital room for over a decade and had not, even once, been able to leave that space. In fact, the first time in all those years her scenery changed was when she was wheeled to a larger room for the interview with us.

Her body was twisted like an old apple tree. Her spine had turned against her and while keeping her in the lying position, forced her to bend like a broken branch in bed. She had what I learned were called "swan fingers" because they were bent upwards in that strangely lovely way of a swan's neck. On a human hand, it only looked painful.

On top of all her physical and legal difficulties, the lawyer – who had been her friend and by her side through the losing court battle to win *her* the right to die – had now committed suicide himself.

I didn't know what to expect the first time we met. Her new lawyer had said that she could be difficult, but I thought, well, who could blame her? We were both a bit wary the first time I just stopped in to say hello in her old room and to confirm the plans for our interview the next day.

But there was something about her which I liked almost immediately. It was in the twinkle of her eye and her spirit which, through all the torment she'd endured, still revealed little bits of itself in her stories and in her smile.

The next day I stood beside her bed, wheeled into the larger conference room, and we talked about her life quite intimately, even as we were surrounded by the crew and various hospital types and her lawyer.

I certainly hadn't planned and had no idea the following exchange was going to take place as we finished our conversation.

"You know what, Elizabeth?"

"What?"

"I know we've just met, but I really like you."

"Well, I like you too."

"I don't want you to die."

"Ah, you'll get over it!"

We both laughed and knew that something had just happened between us. I loved the moment and wanted to use it in the program, but I knew that meant re-creating my part for the re-asks.

What had been a completely spontaneous and emotional response on my part had now become an actor's script for a piece of theater. The problem was not that I couldn't do it, but the fact that I did it not only well, but convincingly. I knew at that moment, it was time to leave television.

As that fellow in Romania had said to me, "You don't begin a democracy with lies." I wanted to try to lead what Bob Coles had called an "honorable and decent life." Play-acting and the other B.S. of television (the capital letters are earned) could no longer be part of the plan.

I figured I couldn't begin whatever the next move was going to be by feeling like I was always selling out. First, I simply needed time to digest the experiences from *Man Alive* and second, I wanted to arrive at some basic truths and real directions for my life.

THIRTEEN

SILENCE

A National Film Board crew followed us through a *Man Alive* production shoot one afternoon and then sat me down for a quick interview.

As usual, I was an abysmal guest, and the *Man Alive* producer later told me that the NFB interviewer had said that I acted like a caged animal. In fact, I felt in television more like the poor wild animal caught against the concrete median of a highway guaranteed to get squashed whichever way he turns. The one in the cage at least has some protection, but I got the point.

Once I "escaped" from television's golden handshake, the overwhelming feeling I had was one of relief. At the same time, I knew that Louise Lore had been right when she said at the very outset that *Man Alive* would change my life. My experiences at *Man Alive had* changed my life. Just not in the way she or I had thought.

It left me questioning the role of the media in our lives collectively, but more acutely, in my own. I had been making my living in broadcasting since 1971, but the very simple truth is, it had lost its hold on me. I'm not sure how that happened, only that it was a silent and slow process.

As I've never been able to do anything only half-engaged in my life, I now knew that it was time for a change. It took a while, but I came to understand that you don't know how steep that career cliff is until you're perched on the every edge and take a long look down. As I gazed into the canyon of unemployment, I was quite amazed to discover how much my life had been connected to my job.

I certainly hadn't set out to let that happen, but I'm discovering some comfort in numbers. I meet more people today who, like me, started a career 25 years or so ago, and now find themselves feeling professionally empty. The hole that the job filled for so many years is either getting larger, changing shape, or doing some combination of both. Whatever the reason, the satisfaction which once came with the work is greatly diminished.

Although my original passion was not television, I had been seduced by it and had almost started to think it was where I belonged before I made my escape. Even today, the memories are shaded lightly by disappointment in the sense that I don't think I accomplished what I might have.

This *promise* of television, for me, is its most powerful characteristic.

Perhaps, like a cigarette package, every television set sold should carry a warning sticker on the side: "Danger! Continued Use of This Product Will Stunt Your Growth." In the middle of what has been a tremendously challenging transition for me, I burst out laughing one night when something in my new place in rural Quebec reinforced this idea.

There is a large barn by my new house which was home to three cats when I arrived with my own two, plus two dogs. If this were school, my guys would be the ones wearing gray flannel shorts and blazers compared to the three dropout trouble-makers in the barn.

When they weren't out on their Harleys, I'd hear them swearing and see them smoking recklessly, leaning against the barn door, flipping crunchies in the air and not even caring that stray ashes were singeing their ripped leather outfits.

As this Quebecois rough and readiness unfolded before their growing eyes, my guys, from behind the safety of the kitchen window screen of course, looked like Norman Bates' mother on a bad day in the basement.

When darkness fell each night, that same screen would be the only thing preventing World War III as the ruffians would saunter over to where they had obviously been fed by the previous tenants.

I tried to catch the three and find new homes for them, not only to prevent the inevitable 12 rounders I knew would be on the card when everyone met to compare notes without a screen between them, but also because I needed some sleep.

With the help of a very generous vet in town, I managed to move two of the delinquents to new farms, but like the one good guy caught running with the wrong crowd, the third one had shown a little promise that, given the opportunity, he wanted to turn his life around.

It is not hard for any animal to endear itself to me and although this last remaining member of the gang wouldn't let me get close enough to touch him for a long time, I was grow-ing quite fond of his presence. Finally, through food, we met and I named him Jackson.

All Jackson had ever known was barn life and survival, so when he first came inside the house, every day was Christmas morning with Aristotle Onassis for him.

One night, as he luxuriated on a rug in the kitchen by the bowls of food he still couldn't quite believe were always full, he saw me sit on the couch in the living room and decided he could do with a little more loving, which he also couldn't quite believe was always there.

The timing was unintentional, but perfect. Just as he waltzed in front of the large television I have, I turned it on. The crackle of the screen coming to life sent good old Jackson screaming and simultaneously jumping three feet in the air.

Before even landing, his tail had puffed up, the nails were out, and he hissed his readiness to fight with this new electronic monster upon hitting the carpet again. Very smart cat, I thought. We should all be so wary of that glow in the corner.

I tried for weeks to get my cats – Boris and Spike – to accept Jackson, but they wanted less than nothing to do with him. I found a new home for him, but it was a sad day when he left.

I mentioned that this transition in my life had been "tremendously challenging." It may be one of the few times I can be accused of understatement.

I paid a huge emotional price for this move when I lost my precious cat Tracks. Having her simply vanish into thin air would have been one thing, but I found her remaining skeleton after she'd been eaten by a fox.

If you have an attachment to an animal, you'll know what that was like for me. If you don't, I couldn't begin to explain it all.

She had been abandoned as a kitten and was found on the railroad tracks near my old home. Understandably, she trusted little in her life, but I took great satisfaction in knowing that after five years, she was beginning to think that I might be trustworthy.

As if she had a sense of how violently her life would end, she spent her years lapping up every comfort and luxury available to her. If a sweater was left on the bed, Tracks would find it quickly and curl up in it. She knew exactly where the sun would create circles on the carpet in the morning and would stake out that territory each day for stretching and cleaning.

She could also amuse herself for hours by either lying on her back and watching – upside down – the fish swim by in the aquarium, or by jumping on the rotating office chair, lunging like a complete maniac toward the sides of the seat back to make it spin around.

She was a wonderful soul and I miss her dreadfully. I suppose that may surprise you. All I can tell you is that the only surprise people who know me will have at this moment is that it's taken this long for me to talk about my love and attachment to animals.

Over the past year I've thought often about Lorna Crozier's lovely poem, "He's Only a Cat," from the collection *Everything Arrives at the Light*:

I've been crying a week
over the cat. There are some
I can say this to and others
I cannot. *He's only a cat*,
many reply. I now divide
people into these two camps.
It's one way of knowing the world.
Meanwhile the cat is

at the vet's in a small cage
and will not eat. *Cats*
are the first anorexics,
my brother writes from Calgary.

I keep hearing the cat
around the house. The first time
it's a wisteria pod
rubbing against the window pane
the way a cat will rub
around your legs. Then it's
my mother-in-law breathing.
She's emphysemic and at night
hisses when she exhales.

The cat used to sit
at the bottom of our bed
when we made love
and when my husband came,
the cat would meow
though I was the noisy one,
and sometimes
he'd even nip my husband's heel.
Pain and pleasure, it's become
an addiction in our house.

When I start crying on the phone
my mother tries to comfort me
in that strange way she has.
Animals have it lucky,

you can always put them under,
stop the suffering. I know
she's thinking of my father,
those last months in the hospital.
Never one for understatement
he begged the doctor –
Why don't you just cut my throat ?

At seventy-five
she's also trying to tell me
something about herself,
but what can I do ?

Right now it's the cat
I'm sad about. He's not
my mother or father,
he's not my husband,
brother, mother-in-law,
or the child I never had.

He's only a cat,
and so I write
this poem for him
with my whole family in it
to bring him home.

The sadness over the death of Tracks endures. She was only a cat, I know, but I have been unable to separate losing her from this transition in my life.

I think television devoured me, the crassness of the industry as sharp as a fox's tooth. Where the media in general had once fed me professionally with a grand buffet, nourishing *what* I was, I discovered that the part of me which now wondered and valued *who* I was had been hopelessly starved.

I am eager to speak with those who have made progress on this journey, and find that I have less and less patience for those not interested in it. It's not that I think they're wrong or even necessarily missing out on something – after all, if you don't *seek*, what does it matter if you don't *find*?

At this stage, for me, the alternative to what I've spent over a quarter of century *doing* can be summed up in one word, *being*. It is a compelling choice.

After *Man Alive*, I didn't want just to continue as usual. It no longer seemed the place to deal with the questions in my head and the attraction of celebrity for me, never very strong in the first place, had by now completely vanished. My ego had stopped making such demands of me.

Like returning astronauts, I needed some time after being in another world, for a kind of readjustment and debriefing. I slowly reentered our atmosphere and began to breathe again like other normal human beings.

I was approached to host an hour-long CBC radio program scheduled for Sunday afternoons. It was presented to me as a kind of *Man Alive* on radio in terms of subject matter, and with the provision that this time I would have more control as co-producer as well as host of the program, it took only a few days' consideration to accept the invitation.

I had forgotten, during the ten "make-up years," just how much I loved radio. I fell head over heels for it all over again

starting up *Tapestry*. Now, the ideas mattered again. Now, conversation mattered again, and there was actually a relationship
with the guest and the audience again. I loved every second of it.

By sheer serendipity (is there any other kind?), I met someone whose wisdom and faith have become for me like the beam
from a lighthouse along the foggy shores of her native New
Brunswick. As if the circle was meant to be completed in some
way, Ray Landry, from my CJCJ days in Woodstock, New
Brunswick, called to ask if I'd be interested in meeting his aunt,
visiting Toronto at the time.

I smile now because all I remember from Ray's call is that
he said something about her being a nun and something else
about Zen and meditation and finally something about Japan. I
thought the least I could do would be to take a tape recorder
and go to meet her.

What I didn't hear Ray say was that Sister Elaine MacInnes
was one of only two Catholics in the world to have been given
the revered and sacred title of Zen master. I also didn't hear
him say that she had spent 30 years studying the ancient ways
and wisdoms of the East or that she had visited the jails of
Ferdinand Marcos to help prisoners by giving them hope and a
way to survive.

Ray also didn't tell me that she would become a valued
person in my life.

We talked for a couple of hours that first afternoon and like
the thousands of others she has touched around the world, *I
felt*, more than knew, something and someone important had
entered my life. I'd love to tell you a bit about her.

Sister Elaine was born in Moncton, New Brunswick, on
March 7, 1924, and grew up in a nominally observant Catholic

household with two sisters and one brother. Early on, she showed a great ability and love for music.

Her studies took her to Mount Allison University in Sackville and subsequently to the prestigious Juilliard School in New York for postgraduate work in 1944, specializing in violin.

As difficult as it was to be accepted at the school and as demanding as it turned out to be once she got to New York, she remembers it now as a "marvelous" time, full of challenges and dreams.

One of those challenges occurred as she was standing and waiting outside the studio for her class to begin one day. This young fellow came up and took hold of Sister Elaine by both her shoulders and asked, "There is a God, isn't there?"

Sister Elaine replied, "Well, I think there's every reason to believe there might be."

This young inquisitor only responded that "there had to be, otherwise none of this would make any sense at all," before disappearing.

Sister Elaine never saw this young man again. I asked her, considering all that had happened in her life since that odd meeting, what her sense of that exchange was now.

She didn't hesitate to say that she "wasn't the least bit surprised when that man came up," because she remembers all the students seemed to be on a path at that time and in that place, which led them to consider the mysteries and issues of life not directly related to their study of music.

This artistic side of Sister Elaine, this gift for music she has, seems to confirm what she says of the artists' *living* experiences of God, that there is an integration going on in that creative expression of spirit, but it was one she admits she didn't fully understand until she got to Japan and to Zen.

But before those revelations, her musical ability took her by train across the country in 1946 to teach violin and to perform with symphonies in Calgary and Edmonton, Alberta.

Due to a little nudging from a fellow violinist who made the decision to enter the priesthood, Elaine MacInnes became a novitiate with Our Lady's Missionaries. She stayed. He didn't. I remember her laugh as she recalled how much she hated the isolation from music and even the more general isolation of that period.

She told me she couldn't articulate it then, but she now understands something of the spiritual life. She caught my attention when she said "it didn't have to do, in a sense, with religion," nor with the lives of the Saints or "being Sisters and all of that."

Sister Elaine said that she learned of a source of life within all of us and that this life "kind of gave animation to the whole world." She has spent her life since then getting in touch with that source by moving from ideas to experience.

I confess that parts of what she was saying were a bit confusing to me, but far more important was the feeling of honesty and acceptance and wisdom which flowed from her straight, it seemed, to my heart. Listening to her on that afternoon, I found that I wanted real *experience* in my life.

As a religious novice in the Order, Sister Elaine discovered a book by a Belgian Jesuit theologian named Paul de Jaegher called *One with Jesus*, which, she was quick to point out laughing, "perhaps wasn't the greatest title in the world."

In any case, it celebrated experience and had a profound impact on her still-young spiritual journey, which in a few years would ultimately take her to Japan. She's fond of saying that both she and The Beatles went to the East in the '60s but this decision, like the first one to join the Order, shared a familiar ending. She stayed. They didn't.

She was introduced to the ancient practice of Zen and to the concept of "sitting like a mountain with an unmoving mind." Life in Japan gave Sister Elaine both the opportunity and the wisdom to achieve such a level of awareness.

But it seemed that her time in Japan was coming to an end. By 1973, the work of Our Lady's Missionaries at a TB hospital in Maizuru on the west coast had been so successful they were no longer needed. Sister Elaine, however, was given permission to remain in Japan and to continue, for the next three years, exploring and deepening her experience with Zen.

By 1976, her superiors, wanting to assign her elsewhere but also aware and respectful of her ongoing spiritual work, weren't quite sure what to do with her. In the end, they told her she could do whatever she wanted. What she wanted was to stay in the Orient.

That desire took her to a rural part of the Philippines. If you are ever so blessed to have your path cross hers, I urge you to leave time in your conversation to ask Sister Elaine about the skills she developed at animal husbandry in the Philippine countryside. If nothing else, I guarantee you will hear that wonderful laugh of hers.

But she was also developing much more within a short time of her arrival. She was asked to set up the very first Zen Centre for the Catholic Church in the Philippines, adding weight to the prediction of historian Arnold Toynbee. He said that the meeting of Buddhism and Christianity would be one of the most important events of the 20th century.

Sister Elaine has been a critical figure in forging and encouraging that meeting in southeast Asia.

She would go on to teach Zen to the prisoners in Marcos' jails and although she is characteristically modest about the dangers she faced during those visits, not to mention those turbulent years in the Philippines, they were clearly very real. She faced them with humor, courage, and conviction.

It may not be one of those Buddhist moments she loves, but it does seem that once her work with the Zen centre and the political prisoners in Manila was up and running, the timing of an offer from London, England, couldn't have been more perfect.

She now lives in Oxford as the director of an organization called The Prison Phoenix Trust, which works in prisons around the British Isles with the goal of turning jail cells into places of spiritual retreat and liberation.

I remember her exact words to me during the course of that conversation when we first met. She said, in describing the practices in those difficult first years with the Order, that "I was always called to something more silent."

It was a lovely expression that defined, for me, my own inner restlessness at the time. Sister Elaine made me aware that I had spent an enormous amount of my life in my head – as I should have done, I might add. Although the temptation here to be snarky is great, I'll resist and say only that the brain *should* be the "organ" of choice for journalists.

The choice between using more of it and all the yak-yak-yak-yak-yak-yak noise that goes with that profession, or trying to hear the silence and learn from its vast richness was, if you'll excuse the expression, a "no-brainer" for me.

Here's what a student wrote after Sister Elaine went to Japan in 1984 to receive her certification as a Zen teacher: "It was a moment of joy and thanksgiving, but for those who had studied with her through the last ten years, the sacred stamp of a Zen master has already been manifested through the discipline, generosity and wisdom of this most normal, most ordinary Elaine MacInnes."

Through *Tapestry* on CBC radio, Sister Elaine first entered my life as just another guest. I would be very happy and honored to think of her now as only a new friend, but that wouldn't begin to describe what she means to me. She has become, without any fanfare, a kind of guide for me through the ancient wisdoms and paths presented all of us who search in this life. I cherish the opportunities I have to sit and speak with her and to absorb all that she has to offer.

I could no longer escape the truth, though, that even my first love – radio – could no longer offer me the calm and satisfaction it once did. I've already told the story of the time I asked Rene Levesque if he felt he had been treated more harshly by separatist voters after losing their *dream* of independence than he would have been had it only been another political project, and of his surprising response that the sovereignty of Quebec had always been only a project for him.

While it may be as risky for broadcasters as it is for politicians to express a belief in dreams, I have no such trouble declaring that radio never became a project for me. Perhaps the fall from such a great passion, then, is harder to understand and digest than when losing "just a job."

It didn't help that my departure from *Tapestry* was their decision or that, after 25 years, no one in management had the decency then, or since, to say a single word to me. It hurt a lot to be simply handed an envelope by some weasely bureacrat. But as sure a sign of progress as any, I know that's only my dreaded ego surfacing again. The truth is my time at the CBC had really come down to the question of who would be the first to leave whom.

When I joined the corporation in the early '70s, it had creative juices flowing through its veins. But its arteries are now so clogged by such bureaucratic cholesterol that only dreary and tedious committees meet to recommend further study of the chest pains, unaware of the problems at the very heart of the organization. By the time the CBC and I parted company, I found I was spending more hours hacking my way through layers of people who never actually did anything but administrate than I did sitting in the studio and communicating. And that *act* of communication was precisely what had attracted me all those years ago in New Brunswick.

In some ways, it has been only with reflection that I have a grasp on just how unplanned it all was, but I see just as clearly how the threads of community, communion, communication ran through it all. I know how lucky I was to work with creative and challenging people across the country and around the world.

And as I continue to try to explore a new direction for myself, my luck continues. I need to notice and listen to the silence of life – and Sister Elaine, who knows and generously shares its richness and potential, appears before me. I am enriched beyond measure by this unexpected good fortune of having someone help me find that "inner source of life."

And I'm going to need all the help I can find, because I feel drawn to a difficult journey. One which embraces contemplation in a society which dismisses the value of Sister Elaine's silence. One which profoundly cares for others in a greedy world and culture of lazy simplicities, where the moral compass is more often directed by obligation than responsibility.

I want to have the courage of an open heart that feels and responds in a world which rarely does, and I know that means accepting the mistakes of involvement over the cool detachment of observation. I need to feel connected, as if I belong to this great mystery of our lives. I want to hold out my hand and touch the hands of others, reach for understanding and compassion through the darkness and distance of space. I want my head to be brave enough to be aware of the great cruelties and insults of this planet, but just as filled with hope that one day, we'll learn enough to stop hurting it and diminishing each other.

And I want to forget about television and the media, take a very long, hot shower, and walk with my dogs and cats through the woods until dark. With a spirit that's slightly used, but contented.